THE ENCYCLOPEDIA OF ARCHERY

THE ENCYCLOPEDIA

OF

ARCHERY

BY

PAUL C. HOUGHAM

A. S. BARNES AND COMPANY   NEW YORK

DEDICATION

To my family —
Grace, my wife,
Anna, my daughter,
David, my son.

ACKNOWLEDGMENTS

With gratitude and appreciation I wish to thank those who have aided me by supplying various records and technical data herewith; especially those whose names follow:

Mr. J. Robert Kest, secretary-treasurer of (N.A.A.) The National Archery Association.

Mr. John L. Yount, secretary-treasurer of (N.F.A.A.) The National Field Archery Association.

Mrs. Myrtle K. Miller, Teela Wooket Archery Camp, 450 W. 24th Street, 16-A New York 11, New York.

Mrs. Florence Lilly, who conducts the tournaments of the Olympic Bowman League and resides at 5354 W. Oakdale Avenue, Chicago 41, Illinois.

Colonel Francis E. Pierce, United States Marine Corps, Retired; 1024 Glorietta Boulevard, Coronada, California.

Mr. R. A. Bohning, of Bohning Adhesives Co., Lake City, Michigan.

Mr. Dave Bushnell, of D. P. Bushnell and Company, 116 Bushnell Building, Pasadena 1, California.

Messrs. Sid Herman, R. C. Young, Bernard Novy, and Tony Novy, Jr., all of Manitowoc, Wisconsin.

Also, to the officers of the Canadian Archery Association, and to Rubie and Jack Askham, editors and publishers of *The Canadian Archer*.

FOREWORD

It is my objective to show within the pages of this book a complete outline of archery terms, words and the explanations of each. One will find a great number of these terms put to their true modern use.

Only through a close understanding of archery—one of the oldest sports known to the human race—can one truly realize what a fine sport it really is.

As the bow, the bowstring, and the arrows are the three absolute components which make up an archery set, these three items and their complete nomenclatures follow as basic introduction. A study of each will aid the reader to more easily understand many of the terms which follow.

Although the crossbow and bolt are not generally considered as actual archery equipment I wish to say that this equipment has its place in the hearts of many. For this reason I have gathered and included what information I could find relative to the modern terms of crossbows for this book.

P. C. H.

TO THE MOST WORTHY ARCHERS

I do not believe that any one person or group of persons could pay proper tribute, by a list, to all archers worthy of honor. Where or with whom one would start or finish, I do not know, but I do know this—those persons who will fully carry the load in any club, large or small, to keep things rolling along smoothly are usually the same "work horses" who end up by keeping the range in proper condition for any and all tournaments, etc., not for the praise which is forthcoming for these "labors of love," but for the very pleasure of seeing to it that others will be able to enjoy archery through their efforts. These fellows and gals are the backbone of our great sport and are "selling" archery to their friends daily. The records of its growth over the past two decades most certainly bears this out! Should you have a few archers in your group who seem to end up doing all the incidental work, is it not fair then that these folks be aided by your support? We live in a democratic country and are all free to express our desires; who knows, perhaps your idea may iron out a rough course in a way that many to follow it may do so more pleasantly!

To avoid inadvertent omission of any names of persons worthy of praise, I shall not mention names here, but that archery has gained such popularity of late and that there have been a great many responsible for this success—many who may never see a medal of honor, much less ever own one. To this let me add a suggestion that each person use his conscience as his "medal of honor." Now, I shall direct attention to the worthy ones as I think of them, by mentioning things accomplished by them, not in the order of importance, but so that each shall be remembered.

Let us think (1) of the first target archers who pioneered archery from its early beginning; (2) the early hunting archers who brought about our present-day field archery and hunting regulations; (3) the scientists, physicists, and tackle makers who have done so much to bring about the drastic changes for improvement of modern day archery equipment; (4) the many foresighted archers who worked incessantly for the safety and good will of archery that it would be safe and enjoyable for its participants; (5) of those persons whose donations by way of prizes, trophies and financial aid have injected inspiration and encouragement into the sport. In this latter group, remember the little fellow who gave as a tournament prize a shooting glove, a set of shafts, feathers, or what have you. Those prizes were not to be judged by their monetary value but for the spirit in which they were given. No doubt those prizes were all that the donor felt he or she could afford.

Yes, these people have made archery what it is today—the fastest growing sport in America.

The following few words are intended to give you an idea of how big archery really is to date: (1) There are now 1500 target archers who belong to the National Archery Association, representing 175 clubs in the United States. However small this figure may seem, let us not forget that this association is still largely responsible for the beginnings of organized archery in America. Numbers of students in schools and colleges are enjoying archery on the target range as a credit towards their education, as well as the many community recreational archery activities sponsored by this association. (2) Then, too, there is the National Field Archery Association, a much larger representation, nearly 1500 clubs, with over 15,000 active archers who enjoy both field target archery and/or hunting archery. Sad to say, this by no means accounts for all who enjoy the sport, but is a mere "drop in the bucket" of all archers on the continent. Within these two groups there are and have been a great many persons who, in their own way, however great or small, are most deserving and worthy of much more than the proverbial "pat on the back"!! They have been archery's "unheralded ambassadors and ambassadresses of good will." Give credit where credit is due; it can only lead to a healthy friendliness and many more archers!

P. C. H.

INTRODUCTORY INFORMATION

NOMENCLATURE OF A BOW—SELF OR LAMINATED

1. Tip ends: The extreme end of the bow (both ends).

2. Bow nocks: Receives the bow string loops on each end of the bow. The nocks should be of sufficient depth to hold safely the bowstring loops and should have smoothly rounded edges which will lessen the danger of undue wear to the string loops.

2A. String or nock groove: Has the same function as in No. 2; however, the groove generally pertains to the extension of the nock fashioning along the belly side of either a working or non-working recurved bow.

3. Bow limbs: The working part of the bow.

4. Belly and Back laminations: A belly lamination is the lamination of a bow which is on the inside of the arc formed by the bow, while the back lamination forms or is on the outside of the arc formed by the bow. Note: It must be remembered that not all bows are laminated; however, all bows do have a belly side and a back side, even though the bow may be made from a single, solid piece of wood, plastic, aluminum alloy, steel, or fiberglas.

5. The Bow Riser: The sections of a bow's limbs which increase in depth to make the handle and to stiffen the bow at the center section. The dotted lines numbered 5-A on the bow nomenclature drawing show an alternate type of riser which is necessary to the center-shot bow design. Since it is necessary to cut the side of a bow completely to the center of the bow's width above the handle to make a center-shot bow, it is also necessary to have allowed for this by increasing the depth of the riser. (*See* "Conventional bow riser" and "Non-conventional bow riser" and "Sighting windows.")

6. Fistmele: The correct measurement for any given bow from the back of the bow handle to the string when in a braced position; i.e., when the bow is strung up for shooting. The fistmele varies with bows of different types from 7" to 8¼" and should not be taken for granted. Brace your bow only to a height recommended by a qualified person.

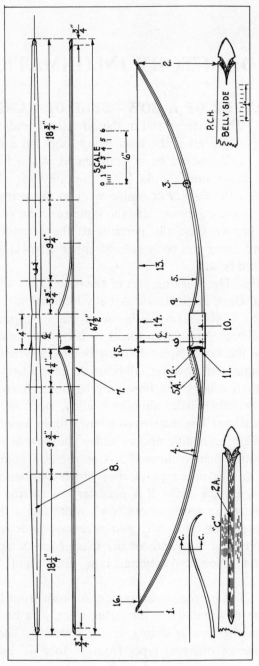

Fig. 1.—Nomenclature drawing of a bow.

7. Side Profile of Bow.

8. Belly or Back Profile: Shows approximate measurements for a 5'-6" bow and the general shape of a modified flat bow with straight limbs; i.e., a bow without recurved ends.

9. Riser Insert: In a laminated type bow the shaped piece used to increase the limb depth for the handle section.

10. Handle of Bow: The center portion of the bow which is gripped while in use. Also called the grip. The dotted lines shown on the two side views of the bow handle grip (Fig. 1) show "form fit handles," and are referred to as "Saddle handle grips." They are further explained under the same heading.

11. Arrow Plate (optional): An ornamental trim inlaid into the side of a bow's upper limb on the side where the arrow passes.

(A) Inlaid plates are usually confined to target and/or exhibition type bows.

(B) Hunting bows may have an inlaid arrow plate or a padded type of arrow plate as a means of deadening the sound of the arrow while it passes the side of the bow.

12. Arrow Rest (advisable): The shelf which the arrow rests upon rather than on top of the hand which holds the bow handle.

13. Bowstring: Although not an actual part of a bow, is necessary to hold the bow to a braced position and to accelerate, push, cast or throw the arrow.

14. String Serving: Protects the string from glove, armguard and arrow wear.

15. Nocking Point on Bowstring: A constant place located on the string so that each arrow is shot from the same position on the string every time. A nocking point is very important to good shooting.

16. Bowstring Loop:

(A) May be on one or both ends of a bowstring.

(B) A single loop string necessitates the use of a timber-hitch on the opposite end of the string, usually the lower end.

NOMENCLATURE OF A BOWSTRING

1. The Loops: The part of the string that goes around the bow tips and into the bow nocks, thus holding the bow into the braced position. (*See* Fig. 2.)

Types: (A) Flemish or corded loop (shown in drawing).

(B) Endless string, bound loops (explained in endless strings).

(C) Timber hitch, see 6, below.

2. (A) The String Serving: The string protection against normal wear. This serving should be (when bow is braced) two-and-one-half inches above the top end of the bow handle and four inches below the top end of the handle.

(B) The serving also applies to a protective wrapping of a bow string loop and the thread used to bind the strands of an endless string together to form the string loops. (*See* making of endless strings.)

3. The Nocking Points: Located exactly at a right angle with the bow string and the top end of the bow handle, or arrow rest

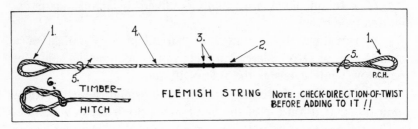

Fig. 2.—Nomenclature drawing of a bowstring.

when bow is strung or braced. Prevents the arrow nock from moving up or down the string when drawing the arrow.

4. The Main Bowstring: A sufficient number of strands of strong thread to hold the tension of the bow it is for. The entire string should be kept well waxed. (*See* "Charts and Formulas.")

5. String Twist: Must be checked very carefully before stringing the bow! If twisted the wrong direction, the string will unwind all parts and come apart. String twist is not always the same. (*See* instructions in Flemish or corded loop string.) Note: If the Flemish loop is twisted the wrong direction, it will come all apart!!

6. The timber hitch, commonly called "bow knot," is shown on the drawing and is further explained under the heading of "Timber hitch."

NOMENCLATURE OF AN ARROW

1. Shaft: Wood, compressed wood,* fiberglas or aluminum alloy.tubing.

---

* Compressed cedar shafts are a patented process of Sweetland Products and are sold by tackle shops under the name of Forgewood and Battle shafts.

2. Point or Pile: The front end of the arrow. (*See* Fig. 3.)

3. Arrow Length: Measurement from bottom of nock to shoulder of point for target arrow, or to back of point or blade for field or hunting arrow.

4. Crest: Mark or identification colors of arrow. (*See* Fig. 3.)

5. Fletching: The arrow feathers spaced 120 degrees apart and near to the back end of the arrow shaft. Note: Since recent experiment has proved that the use of more vanes on an arrow allows for the use of much smaller vanes, which offer less resistance, the nomenclature drawing shows the proper spacings for multi-fletched arrows. Further explanations may be found under the heading of "Fletching." Experimentation has also proven that shorter lower lanes spaced more frequently about the shaft allows for flatter trajectory and more speed to an arrow. (*See* "Fletching.")

(A) Cock feather: Perpendicular to arrow nock. Note: Not necessarily from the male bird but is so named as it stands erect, or at right angles to the arrow when the arrow is properly placed on the bow.

(B) Hen feathers: The two feathers that are next to the bow while being shot. Not necessarily from the female bird. May also be called shaft feathers.

(C) Since the feather angle to the shaft is not an actual part of the arrow, mention should be herewith. In the drawing one might see that the cock feather is placed upon the shaft to a slight angle. In many cases the feather is actually in a true helix spiral, meaning that the feather is actually at a right angle to the shaft at all points of contact with the shaft. It is important to note that if one feather is set to an angle or spiral, it will then be necessary to place all other feathers on that same arrow likewise to be proper. (*See* Fig. 3.)

6. Nock: The string slot at the feather end of the arrow shaft. The nock should always be perpendicular to the flat grain layers of a natural wood arrow.** Nocks are generally molded plastic which saves the arrow when, or if, broken by other arrows. Plastic nocks are easily and quickly replaceable.

(A) Index nocks: (1) A nock which has a small raised rib slightly below the string slot and perpendicular to the string slot; (2) the index enables a person to properly nock an arrow to his

---

** The nock or string slot of a compressed cedar arrow must be parallel with the grain layers to have uniform spine or stiffness.

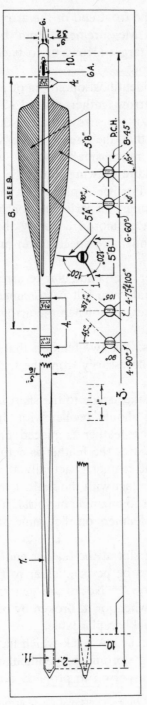

Fig. 3.—Nomenclature drawing of an arrow.

bowstring without looking to see if the cock feather is perpendicular to the bow; (3) when properly installed the index should parallel the grain layers of a wood shaft and also be directly behind and in alignment with the arrow cock feather.

7. Footing (arrow): A hardwood front and applied to an arrow shaft by means of inlay work. A footing is generally applied before shafts are doweled and are for beauty and durability. Footed shafts are usually smaller diameter than self shafts of the same spine and weight. Arrow stability is also enhanced by use of footed shafts. Compressed wood arrows which are footed merely have additional density compressed into the front end of the arrow square before the doweling process. (*See* "Footings, arrow.")

8. Shaft Taper: Usually the latter portion, approximately seven to eight inches of the shaft, the purpose of which is to remove weight from the shaft in a manner that the spine is not hindered to any appreciable degree.

9. Barrelled Shaft Tapers: Same as No. 8, only both ends of the shaft are made smaller to a slight degree.

10. Nock and Point Taper: Tapered shaft end which receives the point or plastic nock when tapered holes are present for use.

11. Shaft Tennon: A shoulder cut on the shaft end to receive either a parallel hole point, or pile, or a parallel hole nock. The tennon reduces the size of the shaft end so that the point or nock is flush with the surface of the shaft.

THE ENCYCLOPEDIA OF ARCHERY

Acceleration of a Bow: The speed with which any given bow will deliver or propel an arrow properly suited to it. (*See* "Cast of a Bow," and "Velocity.")

Accessories Case: A lightweight box designed to conveniently store the accessories and equipment of an archer. Cases of this type vary greatly in size and design.

Action of a Bow: Has reference to the fact that a straight limbed bow's drawing weight pyramids with the entire length of the draw. When released, the string leaves the string hand at its maximum acceleration. As the acceleration of the string falls off to a slight degree when it nears the natural braced position of the bow, the arrow which is being propelled, or cast, likewise decreases in its speed. With reference to a bow that has working recurved tips, i.e., tips which actually unbend as the bow is drawn, the draw has the feeling of a heavier drawing short length bow (than it actually is) until the string leaves the bow tips, at which time the archer has a purchase on the entire length of the bow's limbs; at that time it will be noticed that the tension or draw weight will not increase as fast per inch of draw for the remainder of the drawing length of the arrow. In fact, a bow with working recurved tips seems to soften up near the end of the draw rather than to build up. As the string on a recurved bow is released the string will leave the hand in the same manner as it does with a straight limbed bow; however, with the recurved bow the acceleration of the string increases as soon as the tips return to their natural braced or built-in curve and when the string again has come into contact with them. At this time the acceleration makes a decided increase and the string as well as the arrow will have a definite increase in speed due to the shorter action of the bow's limbs. The forward motion of the recurved tips of a bow aids a bow's action to return to its natural braced position.

Adhesives: For archery use there are many fine glues which have been proven in this field. The proper choice of your archery adhesive, however, is of great importance. The R. A. Bohning Adhesives Company, Route 2, Box 140, Lake City, Michigan, reports that since World War II and the era of the laminated composite bows there are now many room-setting synthetic resin glues available to the home workshop. These may be divided into three classes: urea formaldehyde, resorcinal, and epoxy, of which the latter is the most recent and requires the greatest amount of skill and knowledge for safe use and should only be considered by an advanced craftsman.

Some examples of urea formaldehyde gluing adhesives are Weldwood, Cascamite, and Urac 185. Examples of resorcinal adhesives are Penacolite, Cascophen (Elmer's Glue) and Tox-Tite. Among the Epoxy adhesives are Parabond #100, B-18, and Borden's Epiphen Epoxide ER 823.

The urea formaldehyde adhesives are light in color, reasonably low in cost, and good for gluing of woods of medium density such as maple, yew wood, hickory and walnut. The resorcinal adhesives are more durable and are moisture and heat resistant. Some disadvantages, however, are their dark color which leaves a dark glue line, and their comparative high cost. These adhesives are safe to use with most any type of composite bow construction as long as the manufacturers' directions are closely followed.

The epoxy adhesives are also resin adhesives which are extensively used for glass laminates. These will withstand impact, have good flexibility, and are very tough when cured. Epoxy adhesives are a sure bet when used to glue fiberglas to any of the modern composite bows, especially when the bow core is of osage orange.

Aggregate Scores: Scores which are combined to make up a total for a shoot of two or more days, not necessarily of the same rounds.

Aim: To aim a bow is actually one's ability to properly direct the path of the arrow from the archer himself to the actual target which is to be hit.

Aiming Center or Spot: The aiming center in case of any type of archer's target is the exact spot upon that target which an archer may focus his eyes. Field archery targets usually have a small black spot which is sized in relation to the actual size of the target. In target archery the aiming center cannot exceed three inches and for its use (a) with three archers only, all must favor its use; (b) four archers, three must favor its use; (c) five archers, four must favor its use.

Aiming a Bow and Arrow: The aiming of a bow and arrow may be divided into three well-known classes: (1) the bow sight, which when used is termed "free style" aiming; (2) instinctive or space aiming; (3) the point of aim, which to a novice is the most confusing to comprehend. In the same order as listed, the explanations follow.

(1) *Bow Sight.* An attachment which is attached to a bow to aid an archer to aim consistently. A sight comprises a horizontal pin or bar which may be raised or lowered on the back of a bow, and a piece attached to the bow itself for the purpose of holding the sight bar. As a lateral, or right and left adjustment, the sighting bar is moved either toward the side or away from the side of the bow. An archer who uses a bow sight will first locate the bull's-eye of the target and focus his eyes on it. In his secondary vision he will then watch the approaching positions of the sight pin in

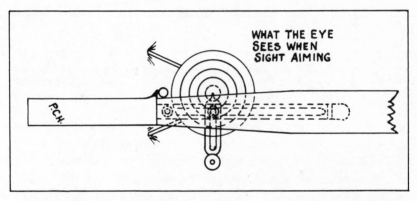

Fig. 4.—This is one of the many types of bow sights in use today and how it appears in actual use. Note that the cross bar pin is dead center on the bull's-eye before the arrow is released.

relation to the center of the bull's-eye as the sight enters the picture; i.e., the eyes are not capable of focusing sharply upon two objects at the same time when they are of any given distance apart, even though they are in direct alignment with one another. To check this, focus your eyes on the end of a pencil point and then try to rapidly move it onto any object in the distance. The object may be lost altogether. But if you reverse this experiment, you will be able to stop the point of the pencil exactly on the object. (*See* "Bow Sight" and "Prism Lens.")

(2) *Instinctive or Space Aiming.* This method when understood is quite simple and very effective to use and is adapted

mainly to field and hunting archery due to the fact that a field target is often moving, thus causing an increase or decrease of distance to be considered. In the opinion of the author there is no person born with the natural instinct to shoot a bow and arrow; therefore, he chooses the words "Space Aiming" which is one's ability to rapidly make an adjustment of the space which he sees

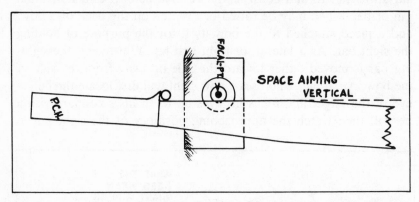

Fig. 5.—This is what the aiming eye sees when shooting without the use of a bow sight or point of aim. This shot would be from a distance which would be considerably less than "point blank" range.

between the full drawn arrow point and the aiming spot on the target he wishes to hit—while looking alongside the bow at the target. With this method a high anchor point is used, mainly due to the amount of space involved for consistent aiming. A low anchor point is more in evidence with a point of aim or a bow sight. An archer using this method of aiming should primarily focus his eyes on the target or bull's-eye; secondary vision will in turn give the position of the bow hand in relation to the target, or the "space" necessary to the approximate aim. (*See* "Instinctive or Space Aiming.")

(3) *Point of Aim.* Many archers prefer the "point of aim" method of shooting a bow and arrow. This method may be briefly explained as follows: After the arrow has been drawn and properly anchored at full draw and the bow hand has been raised to what the archer estimates is the proper height, he will at that time look directly over the arrow point to a spot on the ground as a reference point for his next shot if all is correct. If the arrow falls short, all that is necessary is to repeat this procedure but the next time he will locate a point nearer to the target in relation to the amount

of his previous error; vice versa if his first arrow was too high. The reference point on the ground is called a "point of aim." Contrary

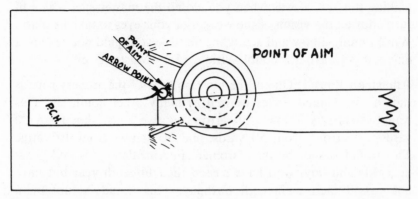

Fig. 6.—Note that the aiming eye appears to see a small clump of grass on the ground by looking over the point of the arrow. Thus the small clump of grass is called the "Point of Aim".

to the preceding methods of aiming, the archer neither sees a sight in his aim, nor the target, but by looking directly over the point of the arrow he sees the point of aim. The eyes should remain focused on the point of aim until the release is completed. There are times when the point of aim might be upon the target, even to the extent of directly on the bull's-eye, in which case the point of aim would be point blank range. (*See* "Point Blank," "Point of Aim" (method of aiming a bow and arrow), and "Point of Aim Range Finder," and "Aiming Eye.")

Aiming Eye: The aiming eye is the eye which actually does the aiming of the arrow. In most cases this will be the eye which the arrow is drawn the nearest to (with reservations): Some archers are able to keep both eyes open while aiming by any of the preceding methods since they happen to anchor under their master-eye (the stronger of their eyes). Others, unable to aim properly, must close the eye which is on the opposite side of the face from their anchor point since they have found that they do not draw under or near to the master-eye. This at times subjects them to seeing a double vision; i.e., they appear to see two images. In this case *only,* the true master-eye should be closed to avoid confusion. To retain depth perception both eyes should be left open if at all possible. (*See* "Depth Perception.")

A simple test will teach you which of your eyes is your master-eye. Point your finger at an object; singularly but alternately open and close each of your eyes. If your finger appears to move while making this test, it was when you closed the master-eye, which in turn allowed the vision of the weaker of your eyes to take its place. While aiming a bow and arrow the master-eye should not be closed unless it is to avoid a double vision. (*See* "Master Eye.")

American Round: One of the most popular of the archery rounds shot in the United States as well as many other countries. This round is shot as follows: 30 arrows or five ends, shot from 60 yards; 30 arrows from 50 yards, and 30 arrows from 40 yards. This round is shot by men, women, intermediate girls and boys; i.e., girls and boys who have passed their fifteenth year but have not passed their eighteenth birthday. This round is shot on a standard 48″ target.

American Round—Junior: This round is for girls and boys who have not reached their fifteenth birthday and consists of the following: 30 arrows, or five ends, shot from each of the following distances—50, 40, and 30 yards—on a standard 48″ target.

Anchor Point: An archer's anchor point is the place upon or against his face where he holds the hand which in turn has drawn the bow string. The anchor point must be precisely located each time an arrow is drawn if the arrows are to be shot consistently as planned.

(1) The under-eye anchor point means that the arrow has been drawn directly under the aiming eye and this enables this eye to easily see if the arrow is actually aimed toward the target or if it is at a slight angle and may perhaps miss the target.

(2) The center of the chin anchor allows the master eye to do the actual aiming and in this case the point of aim or the sight must be adjusted to compensate for the error if there is one. Note: Please see the reservations for the "Aiming Eye" and "Triangulation (in archery)."

Anti-coagulant: All hunting archers are faced with the problem of inflicting critical injury to their pursued game with the possibility of losing their quarry due to a poor blood trail. For this reason the author has inquired into the use of an anti-coagulant which can be used on hunting heads. With reasonable caution against self-inflicted injury, this solution is not necessarily danger-

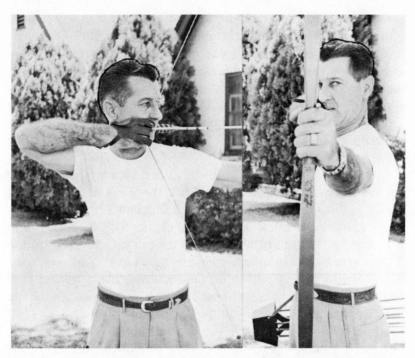

Front and side view of the under-eye anchor point. This is a high, or cheek, anchor and is commonly used by many field archers and hunters.

This is a low, center, or point of the chin anchor with the thumb under the chin. Many target archers anchor to the side of the chin and place their thumb up and along the side of the cheek, while others, even though anchoring at the side of the chin, place the thumb directly behind the jawbone. These are termed "target archery anchors."

ous. Its use will prove to induce bleeding freely and will help to assure the recovery of injured game.

(A) Make a saturated solution of Sodium Citrate Crystals, about one tablespoonful to one half cup of water. (B) Dip each of the sharpened blades into this solution and allow to dry. *Do not wipe dry!* After coating hunting heads with an anti-coagulant these arrows should be carried in a quiver which holds each arrow separately from another so that the coating is not disturbed prior to the arrow's use. (*See* "Quivers.")

Caution: As a safety measure, where an archer may accidentally cut himself with a blade treated with the preceding solution, a person should carry a small bottle of Calcium Chloride solution as an antidote and a few gelatin sponges which must be applied to the wound after it is first washed with the calcium chloride. In case of a severed vein or artery, the use of a tourniquet would be necessary. In case of self injury caused by a blade treated with Sodium Citrate, a physician should be consulted regardless of any field treatment.

Note: Consult your local game laws and warden to be sure that there is no law forbidding the use of anti-coagulants, as just explained, in the area where you plan to hunt! (*See* "Curara.")

Arbalest: A medieval weapon (a cross bow) which comprises of a short stout bow which is mounted horizontally and at a right angle to the forward end of a short gun type stock. The bow was usually of such extreme drawing weight that it required a mechanical cocking device. (*See* "Crossbow.")

Archer: One who enjoys the art of shooting a bow and arrow either for the sole sport of competition, for relaxation, or for actual hunting with bow and arrow. An archer is also a bowman and an archer who hunts with a bow and arrow is called a bowman hunter. (*See* "Bowman" and "Bowman Hunter.")

Archers Paradox: (*See* "Paradox Archers.")

Archery: The actual sport of shooting a bow and arrow. Archery and the use of the bow and arrow as a means of subsistence date back for many centuries and is considered as second only to the wheel in importance to man. Today archery is divided into two main classifications: (1) Target archers who enjoy the sport mainly for the competition and friendly association with others, and (2) The field archers and hunters who enjoy archery as a competitive sport and also as a means of taking legal game as well as predators.

Archery Associations: Basically there are two main bodies of archers which function in the United States of America. They are the National Archery Association (N.A.A.), fostering target archery, and The National Field Archery Association (N.F.A.A.), which fosters field archery and hunting. (*See* "Associations, National.")

Archery Golf: This game is played with different rulings as to target size, method of scoring and the type of equipment which is permissible to use. The basic idea, however, is the same everywhere it is played, which is roughly as follows: (1) The use of a target bow, (or sometimes a flight bow is also used), target or field arrows, several small round targets about 12″ in diameter, a like number of target faces having a 4″ bull's-eye, an 8″ ring and the outer ring 12″. (2) A golf course and golfers who like the idea of a match of this kind. (3) The targets should be placed on the green several feet from the regular hole. (4) All shots at the target to "putt or hole out" must be made from a distance of ten yards. (5) In "putting," if the archer fails to hit the bull's-eye and goes into the first ring therefrom, his score is increased by two points; if the arrow goes into the outer circle, it is increased by three points; a bull's-eye will add only one point to the score up to the green. (6) Otherwise this game is played with bow and arrow against golfers, scoring one additional point for each shot taken. (7) If this round is to be a popular one, the rules must be such that the better archers will have to be on their best game to win; otherwise, the golfers won't ask for a second round of it!!

Archery Magazine: The official organ of the National Field Archery Association of the United States of America. This magazine deals mainly with roving, field and hunting archery. Stories submitted by many of its readers make up a fair portion of its contents monthly. There are articles which cover local, state and national tournaments, as well as game laws. There are many articles of a tackle making nature. This magazine may be obtained in conjunction with your affiliation into the National Field Archery Association (N.F.A.A.) whose mailing adress is P. O. Box 388, Redlands, California. (*See* "Magazines, Archery.")

A beautiful background for a target tournament, The Stanley Park's Brock-
ton Oval, Vancouver, B. C. The path which leads to the top of the mountain
in the background is a ski-chair lift on Grouse Mountain. The Greenwood
Archers field course is just beyond the fir tree in the right. (Photo courtesy
of Whitefoot Studio, Vancouver, B. C.)

Archery Ranges: As in associations there are two basic types of
ranges which are the target archery range and the field archery
range. The latter, by minor changes, is adaptable to varied types
of rounds.

(1) The target range: Target archery is played on a level field
that is usually planted to lawn and is well kept. If planted to trees,
it adds considerably to the comfort and enjoyment of the archers.
(A) The targets must be at the north end of a target range so that
the archers shooting from the south have the sunlight at their
backs. At no time is it acceptable to have the range so situated
that the line from the archer to the target will vary more than a
45° angle from the north. (B) There should be a space of not less
than ten feet from the center of an end target to the edge of the
field. (C) There should be no rocks or obstacles on the field which

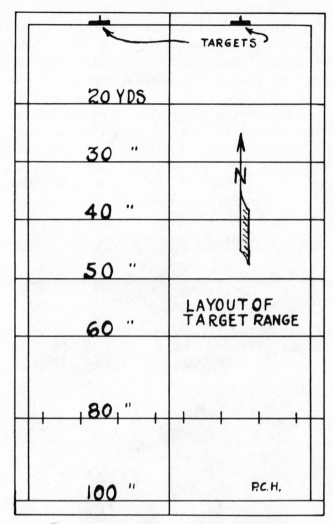

TARGETS

20 YDS

30 "

N

40 "

50 "

LAYOUT OF
TARGET RANGE

60 "

80 "

100 "

P.C.H.

Fig. 7.—Basic layout for a target archery range.

could cause undue damage to arrows which miss a target. (D) There should either be a suitable bunker or backstop behind the targets or a space of approximately twenty yards. (E) All shooting lines should be within four inches of width and must be parallel to the target face, or to a line of targets. These lines must be measured from a point which is exactly under the center of the gold on the target face. (F) The targets to be safely spaced should be fifteen feet from the center of one target to the center of the next, etc. (G) The shooting lanes should be equally spaced between the targets and perpendicular to the shooting and target lines. The lanes may be marked if desired. (H) A suitable line from the center of each target to all shooting lines should be in evidence. These lines may be chalked, pegs, or a mowed strip. (I) The shooting area should be considered as not less than six feet from a shooting line which is being used and spectators must stay behind this area. (J) In the case of the tackle area, it should be well behind the shooting area. (K) In large tournaments, every fifth target should have a wind flag which would be visible from 100 yards to determine the direction of the wind. These flags should be between three and twelve feet above the top of the target and directly behind the target.

Varied targets on two different field ranges on the North American Continent. Aiming a downhill shot on an N.F.A.A. approved roving range near Visalia, Calif., are the author's wife and son. Targets of this nature will help the archer familiarize himself with actual hunting terrain.

This woodland scene shows the 27th target of the York County Bowman range near Auroa, Ontario, Canada. (Photo courtesy of Clifford R. Fox)

(2) Field Range: Every archer, target archer, hunter, or an outright beginner should at some time or another experience the pleasure of shooting around a roving range. Be it only a short five, six, seven or eight target course which lacks many of the preferences of experienced field shooters, the time will be well spent. Although the field range is not as easy as shooting regular target archery on a nicely kept range, the field or roving range will offer many interesting challenges to one's skill.

In many respects a field range could be compared to a golf course and its sand trap hazards, short shots, long shots, and intermediate distances. It is actually a simulated hunting area with the rapid changes from extremely short to long shots, no two remotely alike. The most interesting ranges are not necessarily in the mountains. A heavily wooded area offers deceptive shadows from leaves, limbs or trunks which are parallel to the hazards one will encounter while actually hunting.

A field range is one which is difficult to maintain if built upon public property such as a park area. A natural range with trees, lakes or creeks, flat or mountainous, will usually be ideal if such a place is available and not covered with brush or rocks.

If after spending a short time on a field or roving range, you find that you have enjoyed this type of archery, you may find a group of archers who may wish to make a range that will pass the approval of the N.F.A.A. officials. An approved range may be used for National tournament competition and if a range is to be made, it may as well be a safe one, and one which is correctly planned. An official N.F.A.A. range shall be as follows: (A) 14 targets, distances and faces as follows: 15, 20, 25, and 30 yards, shooting at a 12-inch target face, four arrows to be shot from each distance; (B) 40, 45 and 50 yards, shooting at an 18-inch face, four arrows to be shot from each distance; (C) 55, 60 and 65 yards, shooting at a 24-inch face, four arrows also from each distance. (D) The following must be four position targets from which one arrow shall be shot at each distance, or four arrows from the same position at four different targets: 30, 35, 40 and 45 yards at an 18-inch target; 50, 60, 70 and 80 yards at a 24-inch target; 20, 25, 30 and 35 feet at a 6-inch target. (E) The variation is not to exceed 5% on any target and must be made up on another target of the same 14-target unit. (F) Any type or kind of a bow is permitted except a cross bow. Any type of target or

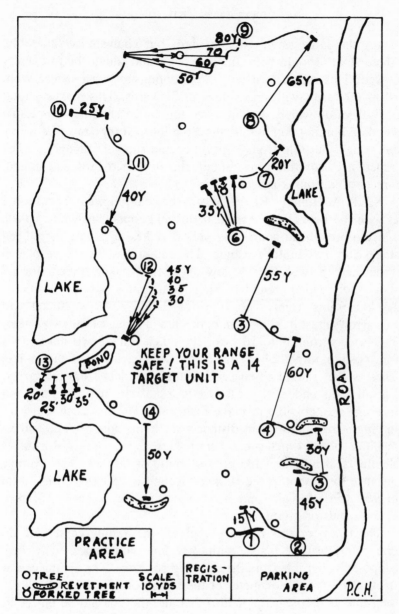

Fig. 8.—*A layout idea for a 14-unit roving range.*

field arrow may be used except broadheads or an arrow which would offer unreasonable damage to the target faces and/or the target butts. (*See* also, "N.F.A.A. Rounds.")

N.F.A.A. Broadhead or Big Game Range: By the use of the same range explained for the field round and a few additional stakes the same range can be used, but changed considerably. These stakes should be a different color and should be frequently moved. This range must have 28 shooting positions spaced from 10 to 60 yards, with an average of 30 yards. This makes a total of 840 yards which should cover the entire shooting range. To simulate hunting conditions, the Broadhead Range must be tricky and tough, but safe from a spectator and shooter standpoint. The target faces for this range should be full sized bird and animal targets of various kinds and sizes.

N.F.A.A. Hunter's Range: Again the field range can be adjusted as with the Broadhead Range. If the field course has white stakes, and the broadhead course has yellow stakes, it is wise to use red stakes for the Hunter's Range. The red stakes should be placed somewhere between the yellow and white stakes, except for all short shots which should be shot from four separated positions. All long shots from 55 to 70 yards should have two stakes and two arrows must be shot from both sides of either of the two stakes. The targets from 30 to 50 yards should each have two stakes for a four position target. Shoot one arrow from each side of each stake. These stakes should be spaced unequal distances from the target. For all shots under 30 yards, use four stakes which are staggered in every way possible to make them safe. The stakes should vary in length for the different distances as, long shots 30-inch stakes; medium shots 24-inch stakes; short shots 12-inch stakes. All stakes should be driven into the ground about six inches. The average distance to be shot in the Hunter's Round is 35 yards with a total of 980 yards for all combined targets, not to exceed a variance of 5%, plus or minus.

The faces for this round except for the aiming center are all one color, usually black, with very fine white lines, which are supposedly invisible from the shooting positions. The aiming center is usually $\frac{1}{6}$ of the diameter of the target, otherwise the faces are the same as used for the field round and they should be placed at the same approximate distances.

Archery Shops and Suppliers: (*See* pages 184-194.)

Armguard: This accessory is used as a protector from the bow string slapping the forearm of the hand holding the bow. Some do not use an armguard but most archers prefer the safety it assures.

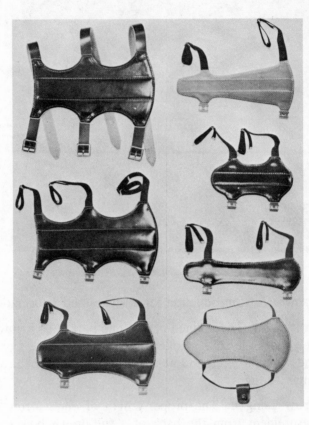

Some of the many armguards which are available to the archers. (Photo courtesy of Bear Archery Co.)

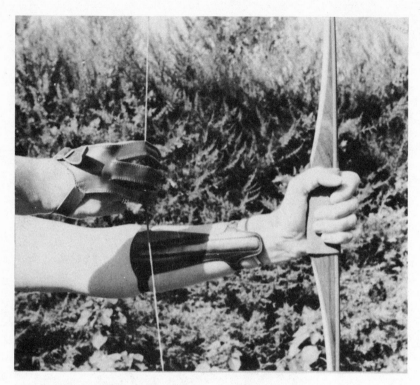

The armguard as it is intended to be worn.

Arrow: (*See* Introduction for all types and information.)

Arrowhead: The pointed or fore end part of an arrow made separately from the shaft. Collector's items are made from flint, jade, hand-wrought steel, and obsidian. These points or heads are made of many designs.

Arrow Length: The proper length of one's arrow is found by measurement from the back of a full-drawn bow to the anchor point at the face. (*See* "Charts and Formulas.")

Arrow Nock: The arrow nock is the extreme back end of the arrow which is fashioned to receive the bowstring. Arrow nocks may either be of self or replaceable design. (*See* arrow nomenclature drawing in Introduction, "Nocks, Replaceable Arrow" and "Self Nocks.")

Arrow Pile: The arrow point is called a "pile" and "parallel pile" both of which are somewhat obsolete expressions used to define a

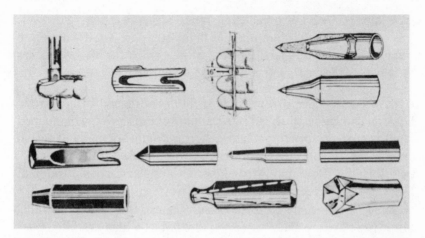

Fig. 9.—*Arrow Nocks, Field points and Parallel Piles or Points: Top row—The warrior nock; parallel and tapered hole field point; regular field point with parallel or tapered hole. (courtesy of Warrior Mfg. Co.); second row—(left to right) Bear speed nock, Bear parallel pile, Bear field point and Bear Blunt. (Courtesy of Bear Archery Co.); third row—(left) Field point (tapered hole) by Ace Archery Tackle Co.; (center) Tapered hole field point by Cliff Zwickey; (right) concaved nose blunt, by Ace Archery Tackle Co.*

regular type of target arrow point. They are usually made from round rods of steel or brass on an automatic lathe; however, there are also points of this same type which are molded from plastic and alloys. (Note: plastic points were used during the last World War due to the steel shortage.) This type of point has a hole which is bored or molded parallel to its outer sides, and the sides are parallel to each other up to the bevel of its sharp, conical-shaped end. The bore or hole of a point of this type is usually $\frac{1}{32}$ of an inch smaller than the outside diameter of the point stock; thus a $\frac{5}{16}$ inch point would usually require that the shaft size be reduced to $\frac{9}{32}$ of an inch on the point end; i.e., provided that the outer surface of the point and shaft are to be flush with one another. When a shaft is reduced in size to receive a point in this manner it is called a shaft tennon. (*See* "Tennon" and "Tennon Tool.")

Arrow Plate: A decorative and/or useful piece of material either attached to the upper portion of the bow's limb immediately above the handle or inlaid into the bow. Arrow plates may be made from mother-of-pearl, leather, cropped feathers, or sheep wool, depending upon the use for which they are intended. Target bows often have any one of the preceeding types of arrow plates; however, it is often found that hunting and flight bows are fitted with sheep wool or cropped feathers. It is the fitting which the arrow touches as it passes the bow, rather than the actual side of the bow.

Arrow Points: An arrow point is the forward end of an arrow; however, not necessarily an integral part of the arrow. An attached point is an accessory to an arrow. Arrow points are many in design as may be seen by the pictures "Arrow Nocks," "Broadheads," and "Fishing, Bow and Arrow," which are listed in the "Index of Drawings and Pictures."

Some of the many types of points are as follows: (1) Parallel piles (*See* "Arrow Pile")—(a) arrow points which are fitted over the forward end of an arrow shaft (used more specifically for regular target archery arrows), (b) Insert type target points are to be fitted into the front end of hollow arrow shafts. These points have a small round rod which continues and extends from behind the actual point, and is reduced in size to that of the inside diameter of the tubing for which they are to be installed. (2) Field Points—(a) have parallel holes; i.e., holes bored parallel to the outer sides, (b) tapered or conical holes, and (c) others have a combination of both; i.e., a hole which starts out as parallel with the outside and is then bored further, with a taper also; the purpose of which is to allow it to be used either by slipping over the end of an arrow shaft in the manner of a Parallel Pile, or to be interchangeable with other points having tapered holes. These three types of points are further divided into (d) field target points, those with pointed ends, (3) blunts, those with either rounded front ends or flat ends, both of which are to induce impact shock, and are for hunting. (4) The Broadhead type is classed as the big game hunting head and they are made of anything capable of holding a sharp cutting edge and point. These heads or points are divided into the following types: (a) bodkin; a slender long point which is diamond shaped in its cross section (stiletto shaped), (b) broadheads; flat heads, pointed and sharp edges, (c) multi-edged heads. Many of these heads are made with the tapered cone type hole or ferrule which renders them interchangeable with others having the tapered ferrule while others have a ferrule with a parallel type hole which is not considered interchangeable. Nearly all states which allow archery hunting have a minimum size requirement for broadheads and these laws must not be taken lightly as they are strictly enforced! (5) The last of this list is the fishing head or point which is especially designed for the taking of rough fish with the bow and arrow. A picture of some of these points accompanies the entry "Fishing, Bow and Arrow," and they are further explained under that heading.

Arrow Rack: A storage fixture for arrows while not in use. Arrows should not be wantonly abused nor should they be left to lean against a wall. Arrows should either be hung up by their points or nocks, or they should be placed in a special rack for arrows in a standing position. If arrows are stored in an arrow box, the box should have a few moth balls or crystals added to it before it is closed up for any period. Moths, silverfish and/or crickets will eat arrow feathers from the shafts if this precaution is not taken.

Arrow Rest: That portion of a bow's upper handle which contains a shelf or rest for the arrow to pass over rather than to come into contact with the bow hand. (*See* bow nomenclature drawing.) The arrow rest is important to good shooting in that the arrow will leave the bow from the same position each time. The same is true of the bowstring nocking point.

Arrow Shaft: The main shaftment of an arrow. (*See* nomenclature drawing in Introduction.) The many types of arrow shafts are: (1) alloyed metals, (2) compressed wood,* (3) fibreglass, (4) footed, (5) self wood. Note: A self shaft is one which is made from one specific material and not combined with another, and a footed shaft is one which has either an applied front end of tough wood which will withstand severe shock beyond that of the actual shaft, or as is the case of a footed compressed wood arrow,* the entire shaft is compressed with the forward end of the shaft compressed to additional density to further withstand shock. *Arrow shafts of this type are patented by W. E. Sweetland of Eugene, Oregon. Note: It is the *compressed wood arrow shaft* which is patented, not the compression of wood alone.

Arrow Types: Arrow types are divided into: (1) target arrows, (2) field arrows, (3) hunting arrows, (4) flight arrows and (5) fishing arrows. The purpose of each is as follows:

Target arrows are basically used for target shooting. They are designed or fashioned with light weight construction usually be-

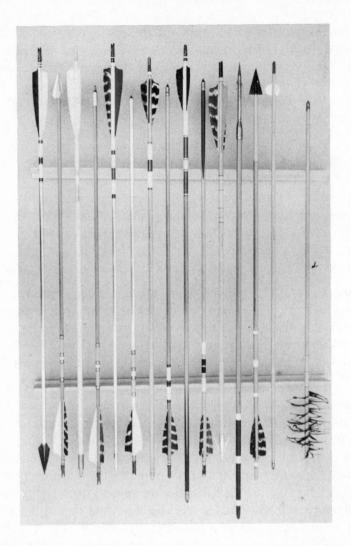

Left to right: Flu-flu or Frou-frou, Port Orford Cedar Shaft; Flight, P.O. Cedar shaft; Broadhead flight, P.O. Cedar shaft; Fish arrow, Rota-Barb head (large), with P.O. Cedar shaft; Fish arrow, feathered, Hill's fish head and P.O. Cedar shaft; Two point footed, P.O. Cedar shaft, (target arrow); Four point footed, P.O. Cedar shaft, (target arrow); Forgewood, compressed P.O. Cedar shaft, (target arrow); Regular self P.O. Cedar shaft, (target arrow); Aluminum alloyed shaft, (target arrow); Aluminum alloyed shaft, (field arrow); Forgewood, compressed cedar shaft, (field arrow); (Fiberglas shaft, (hollow), field arrow); Forgewood, compressed cedar shaft, (practice broadhead hunting arrow); Easton aluminum alloyed hunting arrow.

tween 11 and 13 grains per running inch of total length when finished, which includes short feathers or fletching, points, nocks and crest. A footed and some makes of glass target arrows will run somewhat heavier than aluminum alloyed or self wood arrows. Footed and fiberglas target arrows will be near to 16 grains per running inch of their total length.

Field arrows are used both for target and field practice. The word "field" relating to small game shooting or hunting practice. Because of the additional abuse a field arrow is subjected to, they are made of heavier design aside from the heavy field points, which of late are to match the weights of hunting arrow heads. Field arrows sometimes have longer feathers, from four to six inches in length, which are usually trimmed somewhat higher than target arrow fletching. This of course is to control the flight of the heavier arrows, especially those having field points which match the weight of broadheads to be used later.

Hunting arrows are for hunting and do not necessarily have to be fitted with broadheads unless they are to be used for big game. Small game hunting may require either a pointed or blunt end field point. Otherwise a hunting arrow is designed like a field arrow; i.e., a sturdy, somewhat heavier shaft, long fletching, and some type of hunting head. Field and hunting arrows will have a wide range in weight, depending upon the individual taste or preference of the archer. These arrows will vary in weight from approximately one ounce, which is 438 grains, to 650 grains, depending upon the arrow length; sometimes even heavier with bows of drawing weights above sixty (60) pounds pull.

Flight arrows are of very select stock made with precision and of many designs, but basically they are designed to retain their spine and resiliency and still in a manner which will eliminate unnecessary weight. Flight arrows are most generally of barreled construction, which means "small on both of its ends." Aside from the weight factor, the resistance is also extremely important; therefore most flight arrows have very small vanes or fletching of either very thin feathers or plastic. Little, if any, cresting is used and very small points and nocks are used as the final fittings.

Fishing arrows may be of wood, fiberglas or compressed wood. The solid fiberglas shaft is usually preferred to a wood shaft as it needs no protective finish and is capable of being shot to greater depths accurately due to its weight; however, any wood shaft which is coated with a good exterior grade of varnish or synthetic and equipped with a fishing head is suitable and less expensive. Fishing arrows may be fletched with feathers; however, they will necessitate a protective solution to keep them waterproof; plastic vanes or rubber fletching are preferred. Some archers prefer a shaft with no vanes at all, in which case the attached fish line acts as a drag on the back of the arrow shaft which keeps it on its path of aimed flight. (*See* "Fishing, Bow and Arrow.")

Art Young Big and Small Game Awards: These awards are presented to hunting archers by the National Field Archery Association in memory of Art Young who passed away in 1935. Art Young was one of North America's best known big game archery hunters and sportsmen.

(1) The Big Game award adopted in 1940 is given to those archers who belong to the N.F.A.A. and are in good standing at the time of any big game kills which are defined as follows: Any of the large game animals considered hard to shoot with a bow and arrow. These may include bear, coyote, sheep (wild), goats (wild), cougar, leopard, moose, deer, elk, antelope, lynx, wild hogs, javelina, caribou and panther. However, the big game does not include the young or babies of these animals unless they could be considered dangerous without doubt.

(2) Art Young Prize Buck Award: This pin is identical to the Big Game Award except that it has a diamond added to it and is given to the archer who takes the largest head of either deer species: mule deer, black tail or white tail, in any yearly contest. Rules appertaining to this event may be found in the annual N.F.A.A. handbook.

(3) The Art Young Small Game award which dates back to 1944 is given on a point system for the taking of small game; i.e., a list of predatory birds and animals classed as small game are listed with so many points allowed for each. After an archer has totaled enough points to receive the Small Game award the National Field Archery secretary presents that archer with this award. Small game is defined as follows: Small animals or birds usually recognized as small game, protected or not, or small animals, birds, fish and poisonous reptiles which are considered harmful or a nuisance. Since 1945 there are also Art Young gold and

The patch with the broadhead attached to it is the Art Young patch and the Big game award pin. The pin is made from light colored bronze with red enamel inlaid as its trim. The pin is 17/32" by ¾". The patch is 1¼" square and is of medium weight felt. The layout of the four patches with the broadhead in the center is the Art Young Small game award; these patches when totaled up in point value enables an archer to receive the award pin. The small silver-colored game pin is identical in size to that of the big-game pin. These patches are all 1¼" square.

silver arrows which may be earned after an archer has received his Big Game and Small Game awards.

Artiller: One who makes artillery; bowyers and fletchers.

Ascham, Roger: Famed for his general knowledge of Latin and Greek which was responsible for his being Latin secretary and tutor to Princess Mary and her sister, Elizabeth. His treatise, "The Scholemaster," was published by his widow in 1570.

Ascham is better known to archers for his book *Toxophilus* which he dedicated to King Henry VIII who was an avid archery enthusiast. Born in 1515, Ascham died in 1568.

Associations (National): Within the United States of America the two national archery associations are the N.A.A. and the N.F.A.A.

(1) The National Archery Association has been active since 1879. The main objectives of the N.A.A. are to foster target archery, to make all rules necessary to the proper conduct of

The N.F.A.A. Stump medal, for the winners of the "Free Style division" in the National tournaments, is of gold, silver and bronze for the various classes of the participants. This medal is 1-3/16" in diameter.

tournaments which are to be governed by the N.A.A. rules, (a copy of the N.A.A. rules may be obtained from the N.A.A. secretary-treasurer), and to conduct a National Championship tournament on a regional basis annually, (West, Mid-West, or East) which is open to members of the N.A.A. only.

The Secretary-Treasurer of the N.A.A. is J. Robert Kest, 20212 Bay View Avenue, Santa Ana, California.

The N.A.A. has 1,500 members and represents 175 clubs in the United States. Since target archery is a more formal activity than most forms of field archery or hunting, the latter two groups are greater in number. Many target archers also participate in field archery, and many of the top field archers are spending more time on the target ranges to sharpen up on their technique and personal discipline, both of which are conducive to better shooting ability. There always has been a good number of target archers who were also hunters, but they remained primarily interested in target archery because it demanded more of them.

Because target archery is a more selective sport since greater discipline is required, it is obvious why many archers within the ranks are of a more professional stature; i.e., teachers, doctors, lawyers, and fine craftsmen. Target archery does not require a large area for a target range, and is enjoyed by the students of many schools and colleges as an extra-curricular activity.

A brief outline of the history of the N.A.A. is as follows:

The National Archery Association owes its existence to the efforts of a "hustler" for archery, young Henry C. Carver, of Chicago, who was president of the local target archery group in Chicago in the 1870's. It is interesting to note that A. G. Spalding, founder of the famous sporting goods house of athletic outfitters that bears his name, was vice president of the Chicago archery group.

After consulting with Will and Maurice Thompson, whose exploits in hunting had caused such great interest to develop in the sport, Carver called a meeting which was held at Crawfordsville, Indiana, in the office of the mayor, at 10:00 a.m. on the morning of January 23, 1879. Delegates were present from the following clubs: **The Wabash Merry Bowmen**, Crawfordsville, Ind., **The Chicago Archery Association, The Kokomo Archers**, Kokomo, Ind., **The Highland Park Archery Club**, Highland Park, Ill., **The Toxophilites**, Des Moines, Ia., **The Not-**

tingham **Archers,** Pittsburgh, **The Buffalo Toxophilites,** Buffalo, N. Y., and **The Robin Hood Archery Club,** De Pere, Wis.

The N.A.A. awards two kinds of memberships for unusual and meritorious service to target archery: Life and/or Honorary membership. The greatest award possible for an archer to receive in the N.A.A. is the J. Maurice Thompson Medal of Honor, which is rarely bestowed and is awarded only for significant service to the sport, usually over a span of many, many years. The service, in the latter case, is usually for work which transcends the local and/or regional level of service. (*See* also "Dallin Medal," "Range Buttons" and "Six-Golds Pins.")

(2) The National Field Archery Association of the United States, Inc., (N.F.A.A.) which by amendment 2 of Article IV allows any field archery association representing any foreign country, the Dominion of Canada or its Provinces, to affiliate with the N.F.A.A., and with the same conditions and representation as any State association of the United States of America. Thus, the N.F.A.A. is an International association.

This association has been active since 1939 and its membership has increased to 15,000 active members. Field archery is a fast moving game with a great variety of distances and deceptive targets. It is classed as very informal, in that levity among the participants is very commonplace and rarely taken seriously. Of course, even field archery has its serious times which should not be taken too lightly, such as the championship club shoots or the regional events where all foolishness is kept to a minimum, but still on a friendly basis. Field archery is basically the training ground for the archery hunters who presently outnumber both target archers and field archers by a tremendous margin.

Besides tournament shooting hunting with bow and arrow is rapidly becoming an outstanding sports activity and many worthy tips on it can be found in the N.F.A.A. yearly published handbook. This book contains a wealth of field shooting tips and is available through the N.F.A.A. Secretary-Treasurer.

A brief outline of the history of the N.F.A.A. is as follows: (Condensed from the History of the N.F.A.A. by John Yount, originally printed in *Archery* magazine.)

The National Field Archery Association dates back to 1934 when a small club at Redlands, California decided that "there must be a better way of enjoying archery than by merely shooting at a standard target." Since a few clubs in the eastern states were giving novelty type shoots a whirl, the Redlands group decided to try this, too, but with a range specifically designed for such fun. The first few ranges tried out were more fun for mountain goats than archers, but were so far from the formal range of target archery that they soon became very popular. Inside of a short year there were a great many of these ranges all over the United States.

The targets of the early years were the same as those in use today but the scoring was such that it became necessary to change it to the same as of today; thus the 5 for the center circle and a 3 for the entire outer circle.

Since this was a new game, simulating hunting, it started and is still shot (by a very large majority) instinctively. A few archers enjoy this type of shooting in another class known as "free style or pin shooters"; in either case, the term means a sight shooter.

The target archers within the N.A.A. had their ups and downs, with field archery, but finally in 1940 this new group won its own place and was given the full support of the N.A.A.; hence the N.F.A.A. was on its way.

Michigan, one of the largest states to enter this new organization, gave field archery "a big boost." In the summer of 1940 plans were made for the first national tournament; a mail match and the use of a single fixed pin sight were allowed by those who chose to do so.

The Big Game award honoring Art Young was adopted in 1940, followed by the election of the first officers of the association.

In 1941 the emblem of the association was adopted. "The Old Stump" was designed by the famous artist, Dick Schroeder, and submitted by William Folberth. Without changes, this emblem was adopted by the executive committee.

The twenty pin adopted in 1942 was a great step in creating shooting interest. This pin, designed by the Northern California Field Archers, was used until 1952 when the letters of the N.F.A.A. were added to avoid confusion with similar pins of various clubs.

The Flint Indoor Round for indoor mail tournaments was adopted in 1943. In the same year John Davis, the editor of the field archery magazine, *Ye Sylvan Archer,* was called into army service and the magazine was edited for the remainder of the year by A. T. Wallis when it went out of print. After considerable pressure and a great deal of convincing Roy Hoff took over the publication of *Archery* and it continues as the official organ of the association.

Other events which followed were the Art Young Small Game award in 1944. The gold and silver arrows to add to the Art Young awards were adopted in 1945. In 1946 the association held its first National Tournament at Allegan, Michigan. Although the 1947 national tournament held in Salt Lake City, Utah, was a smaller one, it was represented by the entire nation. This same year brought about the "Compton Medal of Honor," which was awarded to George Brommers, the first member in the association, for his great services, and the "Sportsmanship" medal awarded to "Nubbie" Pate of Barstow, California for his display of true sportsmanship while setting up the range for this shoot.

Associations, (International): Other than those listed as active within the United States of America there are national archery associations in many other countries whose functions are parallel to those of our own.

The International Archery Federation, Internationale De Tir A L'Arc (F.I.T.A.) is composed of most all of the major national target archery associations throughout the world. The "Home Base" of the Internationale varies with the officers chosen to head the federation. For the past several years the federation has been guided by the Swedish archers.

This organization as of 1957-58 is governed by an administrative council whose members are as follows:

Honorary Presidents:
   Paul Demare, Federation Francaise de Tir a l'Arc, Siege
      Social: 14 Boulevard Ornano, Paris 18e, France
   Henry Kjellson, Gumshornsgatan 11, Stockholm, Sweden
Honorary Vice-President:
   C. W. Nettleton, Burnside, Sandhurst Rd., Tunbridge
      Wells, England
Administrative Council:
President:
   Oscar Kessels, 1 Quai des Usines, Bruxelles, Belgium
Vice-Presidents:
   Mrs. Inger Frith, Fairfield, Copthorne Road, Croxley
      Green, Herts., England

Jaroslav Lenecek, Belocerkevska 1175, Praha XIII, Czechoslovakia

Axel Poulsen, Brogade 21, Koge, Denmark

Mrs. Jean Richards-Burri, 255 Emerald Bay, Laguna Beach, California

General Secretary:

Lars Ekegren, Torsvikssvangen 3, Lidingo, Sweden

Treasurer:

Torsten Fahlman, Stureparken 7, Stockholm, Sweden

Other Members:

A. J. Barter, 25 Albert Street, Prospect, South Australia

Roger Beday, 14, Rue Rochambeua, Paris 9e, France

Jose de Fagoaga Laguna, Rodriquez San Pedro 15, Madrid, Spain

Antti Hiekkamies, Punahilkantie 4.B.10., Ita-Herttoniemi (Helsinki), Finland

Robert Neerbye, Bygdoy Alle 33, Oslo, Norway

E. J. Parker, 21 Frere Crescent, Durban, South Africa

H. U. Schindler, Sustenstrasse 12, Masel, Switzerland

The F.I.T.A. enjoys tremendous world prestige and the International meets are frequently sponsored and given active support by royalty. An example of this is that Prince Olav was an official sponsor of the 1953 tournament.

F.I.T.A. is presently working towards the goal of winning recognition for archery as an Olympics sport, and has made considerable progress. The 24th International Olympic Committee meeting in Sofia, September 24, 1957, recommended that target archery be accepted as an Olympic sport.

At the meetings of F.I.T.A., held every other year, each member organization sends an official representative to sit on the Congress, which is the official body that passes on legislation and rules. (The representative from the United States of America has been Mrs. Jean Richards Burri, who was Championess of the World, 1953, and who has also been a frequent runner-up in N.A.A. Championship meets for many years.) Mrs. Betty Schmidt was the official U.S.A. representative to the 19th world meet at Prague, Czechoslovakia, in July, 1957. She finished third in international competition.

F.I.T.A. tournaments are scheduled for every other year, the next regular one to be in Brussels, Belgium in 1958. This, however, is an "extra" world championship. The next regular world championship will be held in 1959 in Sweden.

Those countries represented at the 1957 F.I.T.A. meet as members of this association were Australia, Belgium, Czechoslovakia, Denmark, Finland, France, Great Britain, Norway, Poland, Portugal, South Africa, Sweden, Luxembourg, Switzerland, and the United States of America. Member nations unable to send 1957 representatives were: Canada, Cuba, Germany, Holland, Spain, Hungary, India, Mexico, New Zealand, Turkey, and Venezuela. The following nations are in process of affiliating with F.I.T.A.: Russia, Morocco, Roumania, Italy, The Philippines, China, Austria, Yugoslavia, Egypt, and Eire (Ireland).

All official correspondence to F.I.T.A. should be sent to the General Secretary, in accordance with the decision by the Prague Congress.

Back of a Bow: The side of a bow which is the farthest away from the archer while it is being shot. In case of a self bow, the back will be a part of the stave itself. In the case of a bow which has an applied backing, the backing then becomes the back of the bow.

Backing of Bows: Any piece of material substance which is added to the back of a bow is in turn referred to as a "bow backing" or "the backing of the bow." Backings of bows most common to archers of this day and age are as follows:

(1) Fibre: Laminated paper. Usually applied to hickory or lemonwood bows as a precautionary measure only. This backing adds little if anything either to the cast or to the actual drawing weight of a bow.

(2) Bamboo: The outer hard shell of Calcutta or Oriental bamboo which has been worked to a thickness of approximately $\frac{5}{32}$ of an inch. Bamboo has been a very fine backing but the time involved in preparing it for proper use has practically killed its use. This has also given way to more recent and better backings such as follow.

(3) Fortisan: A trade name familiar to archers of the era of the 1940's; was made up of fine strands of synthetic cellulose acetate. These strands were laid up into sheets bonded together with glue adhesive. Although this product was of great tensile strength,

it soon became outdated because of the manner of its application. (*See* "Silk.")

(4) Silk: Raw silk threads prepared in the same manner as Fortisan. Both of these backings had to be applied to a bow while under tension which is a very good reason why they are no longer used commercially, or by the amateur bowyer.

(5) Sinew (outmoded by silk and Fortisan because of the terrific amount of preparation of applying this backing.) (*See* "Sinew.")

(6) Baleen: Shavings of whale bone. (*See* "Baleen.")

(7) Rawhide or Clarified Calfskin: This backing, while very attractive when properly applied to a self bow, does little for the bow other than as a precautionary measure. Rawhide will hold down very slight slivers and will protect a bow back from slight bumps or bruises. (This backing has given way to fiberglas.)

(8) Fiberglas: Either parallel strands, or of laminated woven cloth, fiberglas has proven to be the most important discovery for archery within the past many years other than the precision matching of arrows. Fiberglas as a bow backing and/or facing for modern composite bows has less stretch, less compression and more tensile strength qualities than any other backing or facing which are known to the present day bowyer, and since there are now several good usable adhesives available for its safe application to composite bows, it has gained unparalleled popularity for these uses.

Balance Point of an Arrow: That place on an arrow where the actual balance is found. The balance point should be somewhat ahead of the arrow's center of length to be effective. Each arrow in a complete set should be balanced very nearly to that of the others of the same set to assure consistent performance.

Balancing Board: A small jigg used by tackle or arrow makers which is used while matching arrow balances to one another.

Baleen: Shredded or shavings of whale bone. Whale bone has been found used as a backing on composite bows. The bone was boiled, or steamed until soft and pliable at which time thin layers of the bone were shaved off. These strips were later glued to the back of a bow much in the same manner of sinew backings.

Bales: Bound parcels of straw or hay which are used extensively as target butts in archery.

"Bare Bow": A term used to identify a bow used without a sight of any kind. The "Bare Bow" division of archers are then in turn those who shoot without the aid of any kind or type of a sighting device.

Barreled Shaft: An arrow shaft which has been tapered to both of its ends, but still made round. This is a common practice with flight arrow construction. The main purpose, of course, is to eliminate weight without danger of reducing the spine or shaft stiffness beyond matching the thrust of the bow for which it is to be shot from. A barreled shaft usually has a bulging taper from the forward end to a point which is about ⅗ of its total length. From this point on to the nock end the shaft is again reduced to a smaller size. The nock end is usually a bit larger than the point end which aids in retaining spine where it is needed the most.

"Base Ground": A feather which has had the feather base reduced to a uniform thickness and width by a process of grinding. In many cases feathers which are referred to as "base ground" are actually feathers which have been precision sawed or milled to a uniform size. In either case, however, these feathers save lots of time when fletching a set of arrows and they add much to a neat looking set. (*See* "Oil Line, Feather.")

Bast: A bast is a target matt or backstop. These matts are constructed from marsh grass or rye straw. Long tightly twisted coils of grass or straw are wound and sewed together much in the fashion of a hand made rug. The coils, however, are not braided construction. Basts are made into several sizes to accommodate the various sizes of target faces used.

Battle Clout: A field archery event which requires the use of broadheads not less than ⅞ inch wide and the total arrow weight not less than 425 grains (13 grains less than one ounce). Six ends of six arrows per end from a distance of 200 yards constitute a complete round. The Battle Clout target laid out on the ground has a 12-foot bull's-eye inside of a 60-foot circle. Other scoring rings are spaced six feet apart, making five scoring spaces with values of 9, 7, 5, 3, and 1 as in regular target archery clout shooting.

Battle Shafts*: Compressed wood (specifically cedar) cedar arrow shafts of a somewhat lower grade of quality than Forge-wood* cedar shafts. Battle shafts are manufactured under the United States patent number 2,182,951 by William E. Sweetland of 2441 Hilyard Street, Eugene, Oregon.

Belly of Bow: The belly of a bow is the side of the bow which is nearest to the archer while in the process of being shot, or the inside of the arc formed by the drawn bow. In case of a self bow the belly is a part of the stave itself; i.e., an actual portion of the one piece of stock from which the bow is fashioned. If the bow has an applied belly or facing (as the belly is often called), it may be one of the many listed under "Bow facings."

Billets: Sections of a log which are either split or sawed from the log in a manner which will render a straight grain to the billet length. Billets are spliced or joined together within the handle section, either by a spliced joint or a steel take-down ferrule type handle. After billets are joined by one of these methods, a bow is then fashioned from the complete stave. Note: Billets should be and usually are taken from the same section of a log, side by side if possible, to insure uniform density and like appearance. It might be interesting to note that since the north side of a tree receives the least amount of sunshine, that side of the tree has the slowest growth and in turn produces the better bow wood, being of finer grain.

Blunts: A flat-ended arrow point used in field shooting as a hunting-type point. The flat end is to exert maximum shocking power of the arrow to the game which is hit rather than for penetration. (*See* "Arrow Points," (3).)

Boat-tailed Shaft: This type of an arrow is one which has its taper all to its point end. The reason is quite the same as for a barreled shaft; i.e., to reduce shaft weight and to retain spine at the nock end where the shock must be absorbed from the bow's thrust.

Bois D'Arc: (*See* "Maclura Pomifera.")

Bolt: In archery this word has two meanings as follows: (1) A bolt of a log, or a section which has been split from a log. This

---

* The names "Battle Shaft" and "Forgewood" are registered trade marks.

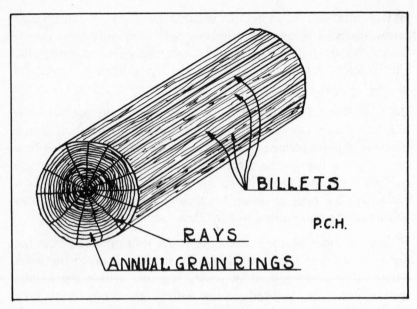

BILLETS

P.C.H.

RAYS

ANNUAL GRAIN RINGS

Fig. 10.—How to locate bow billets or staves in a log section (above); a set of matched yew wood billets which are ready to work (below).

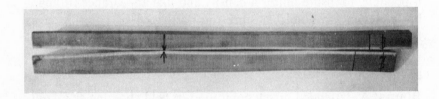

version usually has reference to Port Orford cedar arrow wood in the rough or seasoning stage. (2) A bolt is also the term used to signify the arrow which is to be shot from a cross bow.

Books: Rather than to list all the books which have been written on archery with possible error, it is suggested that the Secretary-Treasurers of both national archery associations have available lists which they could supply at no charge.

Bow: A slat or stave which is held into its bent curve by a string or thong used especially for that purpose. After the bow has been drawn to a greater amount of bend by pulling on the string and in turn releasing the string, the string then transmits the stored energy to the arrow and forces it to leave the bow.

Bow Angle and its Importance to Aiming: In field type, or instinctive shooting, one may notice that many archers tilt their bows to a slight degree. This is to allow the archer to see the target without the obstruction of view, but, one must also remember that the bow may only be tilted to a point or angle which will still allow the bow string to be drawn to an anchor point alongside of the chin or to the corner of the mouth; i.e., directly below the eye. A bow tilted beyond this point can not be properly aimed or shot unless the archer in turn tips the head to the same angle to which the bow itself is tilted.

To further explain the importance of bow angle, it must be noted that when the bow string is held at anchor, or full draw to the face, the archer should be able to take his eyes momentarily from the target and stare at the bow string, at which time the string should appear to center the bow limbs for the entire length of the bow. If this is not the case, the bow must be returned to a position which will attain this effect.

Bow Breakage: Many bows are broken every year by persons who assume that a bow can be drawn to any distance safely. This is not the true case in any sense of the word. One person may have longer arms than another or a person may be broader through the shoulders, either of which could mean a longer arrow.

Safe rules to follow are never handle another person's bow unless allowed to do so and, even then, do not draw the bow until you are certain that your arrow length would be less than, or to say the least, not greater than the person to which the bow belongs.

Regardless of the bow weight and arrow length markings which may appear on a bow (usually below the handle, as 35 — 28, 50 — 28, etc.), a person should think in terms of safety-first and apply the following rules of logic before drawing another person's bow. For a bow which is five feet long, never draw it beyond the length of a 24" arrow; a bow five feet four inches, limit the arrow length to 26"; a bow five feet six inches, a 28" arrow; a five-foot, eight-inch bow, a 30" arrow, and not even to these distances unless you have permission to do so.

A bow becomes "set" to a draw of a certain length arrow. Often is the case when another one half inch added to this will be a catastrophe. CAUTION: Never release a drawn bow without an

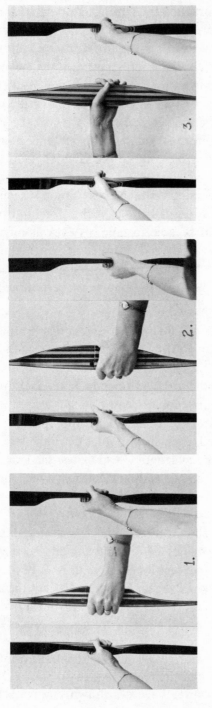

The front and side views (left) of the bow hand grip (explained in part (1) of "Bow Hand Grip"). Note that the bow appears to be at rest on the base of the thumb joint; front and side views (center) of the bow hand grip (explained in part (2) of "Bow Hand Grip"). Note that the center of the bow handle width has come to rest at the base of the thumb and forefinger, and that the wrist is considerably below the arrow rest. The straight wrist (right). With this method of bow hand grip the arrow shaft will be virtually parallel to the bow arm when at full draw.

arrow on the string. This mistake is a common one and has been the reason for many broken bows!

Bow Case or Bag: A cloth or leather bag used to store a bow in while not in use. Every good bow deserves this consideration. A bow case is good insurance to a beautifully finished bow and keeps it looking new.

Bow Form: A form on which laminated bows are made. These forms may be constructed from wood or metal to the desired shape and length of bow. The laminations are placed on a bow form as the adhesive is applied to them. After all laminations are in place the clamps or other means of pressure are applied and left there until the adhesive is dried thoroughly. The bow, when removed, will have the exact shape of the form itself.

The laminations must always be separated from a form with a heavy piece of paper to guarantee the safe removal of the bow from the form after the gluing process.

Bow Gun: (*See* "Crossbows" and "Arbalest.")

Bow Hand: The hand of an archer which holds the bow while the bow is being shot. A right-handed person usually holds his bow in his left hand while shooting. The opposite is usually true with left-handed persons.

Bow Handle: That portion of the bow which is gripped by the bow hand while in use. (*See* "Handle Types.")

Bow Hand Grip: (The manner in which an archer holds his bow in his hand as he is actually in the act of shooting.) There are three basic methods of bow hand grip: (1) Holding the bow in the hand in a manner which allows the center of the width of the bow handle to come to rest against the base of the thumb joint when the bow is at full draw; with this method a light grip exerted by the fingers will allow the bow to come to perfect alignment with the anchor point. Care must be taken that the position of the thumb joint is not shifted with succeeding shots. To hold a bow in this manner, one will notice that (a) the entire bow arm is safely clear of obstructing the path of the bowstring, (b) a very slight movement of the thumb joint to the left or right of the center of the bow handle will correct right or left flight of arrows if the arrow spine is not exactly matched to the bow. (2) Another method of bow hand grip is to allow the handle of the drawn bow to seat itself completely into the "V" formed by the base of the forefinger and the base of the thumb. Archers who use this method (a) usually hold the bow with the fingers closed very lightly about the handle so that the bow is not twisted from alignment; (b) at the same time they must take care that the elbow joint of the bow arm is in a vertical position, otherwise the bowstring will strike the arm at the elbow joint after it has been released. Note: A method of getting the elbow joint in the vertical "locked" position is to hold the bow handle firmly with the bow arm extended, the back of the bow hand up and the bow horizontal to the ground; then rotate the bow hand only, from the wrist, until the bow is in a vertical position. After doing this a few times, one will find that the elbow joint will be easily locked to this (the vertical) position and out of the path of the bowstring. (3) This method of bow hand grip, which appears to be a "tilted hand," or "locked wrist," is quite new and popular and its results seem fine for those capable of keeping their elbow and forearm out of the path of the bowstring. The bow is allowed to come to rest in the same manner as that explained for step (2), but with the following differences: (a) the top of the bow hand is usually tilted into a slight downward position from the wrist, rather than to be above the alignment of the forearm, (b) by having the wrist into this "locked" position, with the bow hand tilted to a slight downward position relative to the alignment of the forearm, and by seating the bow as already explained in part (2), the arrow length will be greater than those for either step (1) or (2), because the bow will then be held to the extreme distance of a person's ability to safely grip the bow for, or while, shooting and the correct arrow length would be the measurement from the anchor point to the back side of the bow. (c) In the case of the regular saddle handle, or the more recent conception, the combination of the "deep saddle" and "palm knob" (a modification of the pistol grip handle), and this method of gripping a bow, only the index finger and the thumb are necessary to actually hold the bow while the other fingers lay against the side of the handle. (d) If the bow has a true "pistol grip handle," the bow is held in the same manner as step (c) preceding, but the second, ring, and little fingers are closed under the bottom side of the grip as if holding a pistol. (*See* "Handle Types" and "Pistol Grip Handle.")

Bow Hunting: The art and sport unsurpassed of taking game, large or small, with a bow and arrows. Many states have now passed favorable legislation which allows the use of the bow and arrow for the taking of big game. (*See* "Hunting, Archery.")

Bowman: One who uses a bow for pleasure as a sport, or as a defensive weapon.

Bowman Hunter: A bowman hunter is one who arms himself with bow and arrows in pursuit of game either for the actual kill or the purpose of stalking the game. (*See* "Stalking.")

Bow Sight: The bow sight has many variations but all have the same basic function which is to make the aiming of the bow and arrow a simple mechanical procedure. The two main variations of sights are direct aiming by means of a movable horizontal bar which is attached to the back of the bow by means of a vertical bar, and the prism type sight which adjusts in the same manner but which allows the archer to include aiming from much greater distances with the horizontal aiming bar safely above the handle of the bow. (1) The plain horizontal bar usually has a pointed end or a peephole, or both, and is usable for distances from ten to eighty yards, depending upon the bow's cast or acceleration. (2) The prism type aiming bar is obtainable in many degrees of bevels for various weights and speeds of bows. Some bows equipped with prism lenses are able to shoot from well over 100 yards and still have the lens safely above the top of the bow hand. Note: The reason the word safely is used is because if the horizontal aiming bar becomes too low or near to the arrow, the feathers may be stripped from the shaft as it passes under the bar.

The first step of knowing where to start is to find the distance which the arrow will be drawn to below the eye, or the exact location of the anchor point. Second, move the aiming bar this same distance above the arrow rest and try shooting from ten yards. If not exactly correct, *follow the arrow location* with the sight bar; i.e., if the arrow goes high, raise the sight a bit and try again. If the arrow goes to the left, move the sight out to the left. When all is found to be correct for ten yards, the sight bar must be moved down the bow limb towards the upper end of the bow handle about ½" to ⅝" for each ten yards that the archer moves away

from the target thereafter. After the sight bar is properly located
for each distance, these calibrations should be recorded on a piece
of adhesive tape which is attached to the back of the bow for this
purpose.

Note: After a person becomes familiar with space aiming and
sight shooting, it will soon be noticed that they are closely related
as the space factor is the same only that in space aiming the distance which the arrow point appears to be below the target is estimated and not determined by the aiming device. (*See* "Aiming a
Bow and Arrow," "Prism Lens" and illustration here.)

Bow Sox: A tubular piece of cloth which is used to cover a bow's
limbs for protection from abrasive scratches and also as a camouflage to a bow.

Bow Stave: A slat either self or laminated from which a bow
may be fashioned.

Bowstring: (*See* nomenclature.) A string which when properly
attached to a bow serves to keep the bow bent or braced and is
the medium of exerting the propelling force exerted by the bow to
an arrow; thus, the bowstring propels the arrow or sets it into
motion. (*See* "Charts and Formulas," steps 3 and 4.)

Bowstring Alignment: This term has reference to the question of
whether a bow's limbs are twisted, or absolutely straight which
would in turn allow the bowstring to exactly center the bow's limbs
and tip ends at the natural braced position or when the bow was
in the process of being drawn. String alignment has a very important part in good shooting, as a bow will not shoot as aimed
unless the limbs will bend without torsion. A bowstring should
exactly center the limbs and tip ends to shoot well. (*See* "Warped
Tips.")

Bow Types: Are many as may be seen by the list which follows:
   (1) Straight limbs. A bow which has tips and limbs of comparative straightness.
   (2) Recurved bows which are as follows:
      (A) Non-working recurved ends, or ends which are into a
reverse bend, but do not unbend to any noticeable degree while
the bow is being drawn.
      (B) Working recurved tips. A bow which even though the

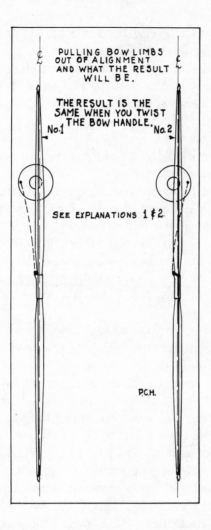

Fig. 11.—*This illustrates whether the result of limb torsion is the fault of the bow or the shooter. No. 1: The bowstring is off center to the left side of the bow. When released, the string will swing back to the center of the bow taking the arrow nock with it; this in turn will start the arrow to the left where it will continue to go. No. 2: This bow will shoot to the right as the string is out of center of the limbs to the right. When released, the string will carry the nock to the left and force the arrow to the right.*

tips are built into a reverse bend, the tips do unbend as the bow is drawn, thus the term "working recurve."

(3) Deflexed bows: Bows which have a slight amount of bend built into the bow when constructed. Bows of this style add to stability while being shot. These bows are also constructed as follows:

(A) straight tips.

(B) non-working recurved tips.

(C) working recurved tips.

(4) Reflexed limbs or bows whose limbs have a slight reverse bend as they leave the bow handle. These bows also are made in the same designs as the Deflexed bows.

(5) Takedown handles: Are adaptable to all types or kinds of bows which allows the bow to be disassembled and carried in a short bow bag or stored in a smaller space than is necessary to store a full length bow. Note (1): Bow types are further divided into the following:

(A) A self bow, or one which is made from a single piece of stock. Solid wood, plastics, metal, as examples. A self bow may also be tubular in its design.

(B) Backed bows; i.e., bows having an applied backing added.

(C) Backed and faced bows are bows not only having an applied backing, but also have an applied facing.

(D) Laminated bows are bows which are made up of more than one piece of material which is glued together. Laminated bows may consist of several different woods and/or plastics combined. Anything made up of more than one substance compounded together is a composite thing. Therefore, any bow made of two or more different components is a composite, regardless of its design or style. Bows (B), (C) and (D) are classed as composite bows; however, bow (D) is a more accepted explanation and example. (See "Composite Bow.")

(E) Fiberglas bows are bows made from fiberglas which has been molded together with bonding resins of one or more types.

(F) Steel-bows. In the case of a crossbow, the bow is a short solid spring steel bow which is tempered to stand the bending and constant use it is put to. As for target bows or long bows, the steel bows are tubular construction. Note: It should be understood that since steel bows are mentioned for crossbows, that a great many other materials are used for the making of crossbows such as composite bows etc.

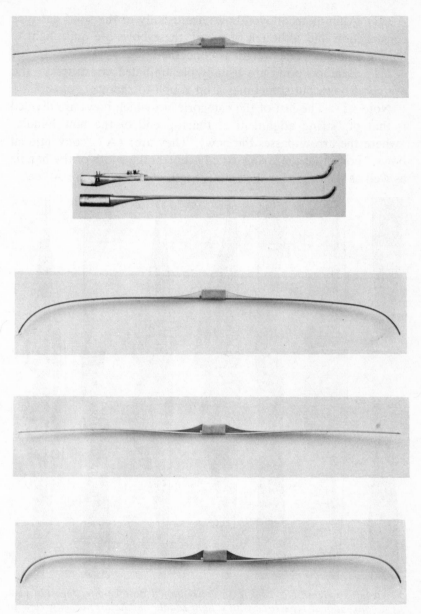

(1) A straight limbed bow. (2) A non-working recurved takedown bow. (3) A working recurved bow with reflexed limbs. (4) A Deflexed bow with straight tips. (5) A Deflexed bow with working recurved tips.

(G) Aluminum alloyed bows are usually of the solid flat type construction and although of metal, these bows are quite light to handle as far as bulk weight is concerned.

(H) Bamboo bows are usually of laminated construction and are good bows but sometimes a bit rough to shoot.

Note (2): The last of the categories to which bows are divided is that of "string alignment at the top end of the bow handle" (where the arrow passes the bow). They are: (A) "conventional bows," bows that the string exactly centers the width of the handle as well as the limbs for the entire length of the bow. (B) A "near"

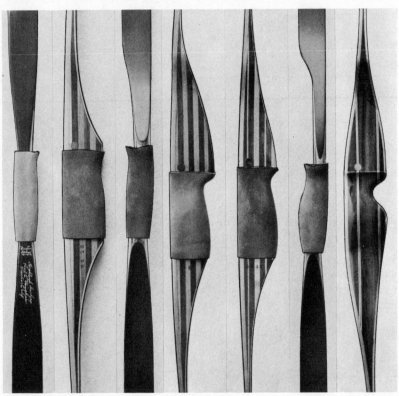

From left to right: The back of a conventional bow handle; the side view of a conventional type riser with a light saddle handle dip; a belly view of a semi-centershot sighting window; the side view of an overdraw type riser with a saddle handle grip; a saddle handle grip without the overdraw; a full centershot sighting window which is made possible by the depth of the upper end of the risers of bows shown in views 4 and 5; the side view of the modified conception of the pistol grip handle with the combination of the "deep saddle" and the "palm knob". This bow is also a complete centershot bow.

or "semi-center shot" bow, where the upper bow limb is cut away to allow the arrow to pass the bow more nearly to its true center of string alignment. (C) The "center shot" where the bow is constructed to allow for a deeply cut away space above the arrow rest which allows for an arrow passing the bow at its true center of string alignment. Note: This cutaway space is called the sighting window of a bow. The height or length that the sighting window extends above the arrow rest depends upon the construction and design of the bow.

(*See* "Sighting Windows," "Conventional Bow," "Near or Semi and Completely Center Shot Bows," "Center Shot Bow.")

Any of these bows may be constructed to the design of any of the preceeding bow types, i.e., an aluminum alloyed takedown bow with working recurves, or a straight limbed deflexed bow, etc.

Bow Weight: A bow's weight means the necessary pounds of pull actually required to draw a bow up to the exact length of the arrow that is to be shot from the bow in question.

Example: A 50-pound bow at 26" means it requires 50 pounds of pull to draw the arrow on that bow to the point of the arrow. For the same token, this same bow drawn to 23" would only draw about 41 pounds of pull. The average 50-pound composite bow actually has a gross handling weight of approximately 18 ounces.

Bow Weight and Arrow Length Markings: Many persons who make archery bows have adopted the practice of showing the draw weight in relation to the arrow length. These markings usually appear below the bow handle as follows: 42—28, 25—24. The first of these numbers will refer to the weight of the bow, the second number is the length of the arrow at which the bow weight is determined. It is usual with bows made for stock, and not to special order, that the weight is shown for a 28" draw. The reason for this practice is that a 28" draw is average.

A bow with straight tips will increase or decrease in draw weight more than those which have working recurved tip ends because the thickness of the curved tips are usually thinner to offset the amount of the curve; therefore, when these bows are drawn and the arrow nears the "full draw" the thin tips begin to unbend with less resistance than is required to continue to bend a straight ended bow. For this reason a straight bow will pyramid on its increased drawing weight, while a bow with working recurves will tend to "soften up" near the "full draw."

A fact which should be understood and remembered is that the markings on a person's bow does not signify the pounds pull of their bow unless that person is drawing the bow to the arrow length which is shown therewith; i.e., a bow marked "48—28," drawn to 25 inches, will require less pounds of pull than shown. The amount will depend upon the type and weight of the bow in question.

Bow Woods: Most common to modern archers are:
- (A) Hickory (should be second growth).
- (B) Lemonwood—a Cuban hardwood is "Degame."
- (C) Yew Wood—of the evergreen family, "Taxus."
- (D) Osage Orange—of the thorn type trees "Bois D'Arc" and/or Maclura Pomifera.
- (E) Walnut.
- (F) Hard Maple (Eastern domestic to U.S.).
- (G) Mulberry.
- (H) Cherry (Eastern, second growth preferred).
- (I) Locust—of the thorn type tree (fair).
- (J) Purple Heart.
- (K) Bamboo—Calcutta or Oriental.

Bowyer: One who makes or trades in archery bows.

Braced bow: A bow which is strung or braced for use.

Bracing a bow: It should be stressed that a novice should never string a bow which does not belong to him without proper instruction and permission to do so from its owner.

There is only one sure way to know in which direction a bow is to be drawn and that is to the direction which will allow the bowstring loops to seat themselves into the fashioned nocks of the bow's tip ends. The bow nocks are fashioned to allow the string loop to go across the back side of the bow tip in a straight line from one side of the nock to the other and thence into the "V" shape of the bow nock on the inside or belly of the bow. In the case of a recurved bow there is a continuation of the string nock in the shape of a channel which receives the string as it passes over the reversed curved tips. Caution: A bow braced and pulled backwards can break immediately.

Bracing a straight limbed bow. This is more easily done if the elbow of the arm which holds the bow is held firmly against the hip and not allowed to move as the other arm and hand bends the bow for the bracing.

Bracing a target weight recurved bow. To brace a recurved bow in this manner, be careful that the lower tip rests firmly against the instep of the foot and that the upper tip does not slip from the hand as the bow is bent for bracing.

This method is alright for bows of heavier drawing weights, but definitely not to be practiced by a beginner, unless one who has been shown the proper method by a qualified instructor.

A novice will do well to first watch a person who knows the proper method of bracing a bow before attempting to do so himself.

The following is the procedure of properly bracing a bow. If no one is handy for a demonstration, carefully follow this method.

(1) First stand with the feet spread 18 to 20 inches apart and nearly parallel to one another.

(2) Turn the back side of the bow towards you, holding the lower tip of the bow firmly against the instep of the right foot.

(3) Grasp the bow near to the upper end of the bow handle firmly with the right hand.

(4) Press downward on the bow's upper limb slightly below the upper string loop with the base of the left hand.

(5) With the side of the index finger and the thumb of the left hand continue to move the string loop up the bow limb as continued pressure is exerted to the bending of the upper limb.

(6) Note: It is very important that the elbow of the right arm be held firmly against the right hip. Do not allow the right forearm to follow the bow or the bow's tip will get completely out of reach of the left hand.

(7) Do not take hold of the bow tip with the fingers which are moving the string up the bow limb as these must be free to slide the string loop along the bow limb.

(8) Watch the nock of the bow carefully and move the string loop only far enough to push it entirely into the bow nock.

(9) Release the exerted pressure on the bow and the bow will then be braced and ready for use. Always examine the bow to make sure that the loops are completely into place in the nocks before drawing a bow.

Broadheads: Are hunting heads for arrows. There are a great many designs in use today. There are flat two-bladed heads, three-bladed, four, and even heads with six cutting edges. One will find that each has its advantages and disadvantages; therefore, as long as one type which suits you will stay sharp and will meet the hunting law requirements in the locality you plan to hunt, that is the most important thing to look for. Modern broadheads are made of medium high carbon content steel which is capable of being sharpened with a good file and at the same time will take a reasonable amount of abuse. Quite recently there have been new heads

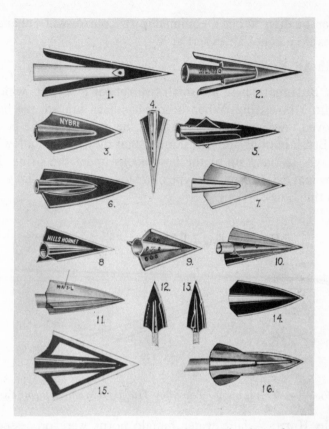

A layout of some of the various types of hunting heads for big game shooting. 1. Eagle's Talon (Eagle Mfg. Co.); 2. Hilbre (Robin Hood Archery); 3. Nybre (Robin Hood Archery); 4. "Bowie" (Walter Bloom); 5. Black Diamond (Cliff Zwickey); 6. Ace Jet (Ace Archery Tackle); 7. Case Broadhead (Roy Case); 8. Hills Hornet (Hill's Archery Supplies); 9. Hi-Precision (Hi-Precision Co.); 10. Bod-Kin (L. C. Whiffen Co.); 11. M-A 3-L (Make-All Tool & Die Co.); 12. Deerslayer (Fleetwood Archery Co.); 13. King of the Forest (Fleetwood Archery Co.); 14. Single Blade Broadhead (Bear Archery Co.); 15. Goshawk (Shumaker Archery Co.); 16. Cobra (Smith Archery).

designed which incorporate the use of adaptable insert razor sharp blades. (*See* "Arrow Points.")

Broadhead Flight: Shooting a hunting arrow for distance. This is merely for the sheer sport of the game and it is the opinion of the author that an archer who excels in this art has to be well trained and with perfect coordination. It is not unusual to see an archer who excels in flight shooting take any one of several bows available and outshoot all others who are participating in the event. The superior quality of one's equipment, of course, will enhance his chances if he is not an expert at it.

Broadhead Round, N.F.A.A.: (*See* "N.F.A.A. Rounds.")

Brush Buttons: These are small live rubber grommets which are put onto a bowstring. When a bow has been braced, the buttons are moved towards the bow tips until the button and the bowlimb meet. Brush buttons are so fashioned that they will not allow twigs nor leaves to hang up at the bow nocks under the string. Brush buttons may be used on any type of a bow and are especially useful on hunting bows.

BRUSH BUTTON

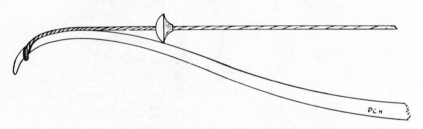

Fig. 12.—This is manufactured by Trueflight Manufacturing Co.

Buffalo Horn: Asiatic water buffalo horns were processed and used as facings for composite bows. The rendering of this type of horn into workable strips required a vast amount of time and the application of the horn to the bow was in itself a project of skilled hands. Bows which have been collected with this type of construction are not only a work of art but those which I have seen in action have a terrific cast.

Bull's-eye: Is the center of a target or that portion of the target which has the highest scoring value.

Canadian Rounds: This round, shot from different distances for each group (Men, Women and Juniors), is a very popular one in Canada. (1) the men shoot the Canadian round, the York round and a double American round for their championship tournaments. The men's Canadian round is as follows: shoot four ends or 24 arrows from each of the following distances—80, 70, 60, 50 and 40 yards. (2) The ladies shoot the Canadian round with the

National, the double American, and the Columbia round. The ladies' Canadian round is as follows: shoot four ends or 24 arrows from each of the following distances—70, 60, 50, 40 and 30 yards. (3) The Junior girls and boys (all ages up to and including 16 years of age) shoot the Junior Canadian round as a companion to the Junior American round. The Junior Canadian round is as follows: shoot four ends or 24 arrows from each of the following distances—60, 50, 40, 30 and 20 yards.

In *all cases* the standard 48″ target face is used for the preceeding rounds.

Care of the Arrows: A good set of arrows will require a reasonable amount of care to keep them good. The shafts should be kept waxed with paraffin; they should also be kept clean and free of old straw which at times may adhere to the shafts. When not in use, arrows should be kept in a regular arrow box which has a few moth balls to keep the moth larva from eating off the feathers. Silver-fish are also great feather eaters!

If the shafts become slightly warped or bent, they should be straightened by sighting them for straightness and lightly bending them to a point which will make them straight.* Warped or bent arrows do not rotate truly and will not shoot as smoothly as an arrow which is straight.

One should never shoot at a target which is immediately in front of a board or masonry wall. Common sense will keep a good set of arrows in shape!

Care of the Bow: Like a set of arrows a bow needs its proper amount of care. (1) One should always see to it that no one who is unfamiliar with archery equipment handles his bow. It is wise to assume that everyone is a novice in this respect until the person proves otherwise. (2) Keep a safe string on your bow at all times. By this, a safe string should be one of a proper number of strands for your bow and one which shows no abrasions or weak strands at any place. (3) Never draw a bow and allow the string to be freed without an arrow. (4) Store a bow in a cool place lying on, or hanging from pegs. (5) Do not stand a bow in a corner and allow it to remain there for any period of time. (6) Keep a bow well waxed at all times to preserve the finish and ward off

---

* To straighten wood arrows, one should warm them slightly with dry heat prior to bending them. This precaution will allow bending more safely.

scratches. (7) If a hunting bow, protect it with a bow sox which will eliminate scratches to the finish and at the same time a bow sox will hide the shiny surface of the bow and will camouflage it.

Cast of a Bow: Bow cast is the term used when referring to the speed which a bow will accelerate or propel an arrow by its force exerted through the medium of the bow string. The faster the acceleration of the bow's limbs, the greater the speed will be of an arrow which leaves the bow, and the flatter the trajectory will be for an arrow shot from that bow.

It must be remembered, however, that neither the pounds pull of a bow, nor its actual mass handling weight, nor the type of the bow entirely governs the speed or cast of a bow. A fast light drawing bow may outshoot a slow bow of greater mass or drawing weight. Both bows, of course, would be assumed to use the same arrows and to be shot in the same manner.

In relation to bow types as to cast, the recurved bow is definitely a faster bow than a straight limbed bow, both bows having the same drawing weight at full draw and all other specifications being equal. The uncurling or unbending of the curved tips of a recurved bow lends to a smooth drawing bow, while at the time of the string release these curved tips have another advantage. Immediately after the release the string comes into contact with the curved ends and the bow then has the thrust action of a short heavier bow and the string momentum increases; thus greater acceleration is transmitted to the arrow; hence greater speed and a flatter trajectory. With a straight limbed bow, the string leaves the hand at its maximum acceleration and never has an increase of speed. (*See* also "Velocity.")

Cedar, Port Orford White: Due to the following characteristics and availability, Port Orford Cedar is the most popular arrow wood in use today: (1) Straightness of grain, (2) stiffness in relation to shaft size, (3) the lightness of actual weight in relation to bulk, (4) the resiliency to bending and the rapidness to which it will return to straightness after being shot from a bow. (5) If shafts are well seasoned before they are used, and if they are straight to begin with, with good care these arrows will shoot well and stay straight for years.

Centaur: A mythical archer with a drawn bow. A fabulous creature with the head, trunk and arms of a man, joined together with the body and legs of a horse. Referring to astronomy, Centaur is found in the southern constellation between the Southern cross and Hydra.

Center Shot Bow: (*See* "Near or Semi and Completely Center Shot Bows.")

Charts and Formulas: The following three charts and formulas are ones which are important to a novice.

(1) The arrow length chart is based upon the fact that the proper arrow length of a large percentage of persons checked has been a very close approximate to 38% of their total arm span, measuring over all of the finger tips. From this, the following chart has been made. Note: The anchor point to be at the point of the chin or to the corner of the mouth, and measurement thence to the back of the fully drawn bow. The first number in each case will be the total arm span, while the second number will be *the net* arrow length to the back of the bow. Hunting arrows with extra length behind the blades must be taken into consideration. Many archers prefer ¾" extra shaft for a safety factor.

48" arm span—18½" arrow, 49"—18⅞", 50"—19¼", 51"—19⅝", 52"—20", 53"—20⅜", 54"—20¾", 55"—21⅛", 56"—21½", 57"—21⅞", 58"—22¼", 59"—22⅝", 60"—23", 61"—23⅜", 62"—23¾", 63"—24⅛", 64"—24½", 65"—24⅞", 66"—25¼", 67"—25⅝", 68"—26", 69"—26⅜", 70"—26¾", 71"—27⅛", 72"—27½", 73"—27⅞", 74"—28¼", 75"—28⅝", 76"—29", 77"—29⅜", 78"—29¾", 79"—30⅛", 80"—30½".

It must be remembered that these are approximate measurements and do not include extreme cases. If your arrow is an in-between length, it would be advisable to purchase the next longer length arrow, as stock arrows are made up to include 1" variations only. If you find that your arrow is too long, it can be shortened, but not made longer.

(2) The finding of the necessary bow length has a direct relation to the arrow length; therefore, the arrow length should be known first. Now the kind of bow, or the construction also enters into the necessary knowledge of doing this part of the selecting; therefore, while this is not a chart, it will fall into the category of a sound formula, or suggestion.—(A) If your bow is to be a self

Three methods to determine your arrow length. Any one of these methods is far better than using an arrow which is in no way suited to an archer. Top—Find the total arm span and take 38 per cent; center—Draw a bow which is actually easy for you and measure the length of the draw. (This arrow is 30" long and has the measurements on the side of the shaft.) bottom—The shaft is placed against the chest and the arms are extended to full length along the side of the shaft. Your finger tips will reach your approximate arrow length. Note: The first method of overall span (top) seems to be preferred.

bow (not laminated), it is safe and wise to choose one which is 2½ times as long as the arrow which is to be drawn on the bow. Example: (Self bow) arrow length 26″, choose a bow which is 5′-5″ *measuring between the string nocks,* not the overall or total length of the bow. (B) If your bow is to be a laminated or composite bow, it is safe and wise to choose a bow which is 2⅖ times as long as the arrow which is to be drawn on the bow. Example: (Laminated or composite bow) arrow length 26″, choose a bow which is 5′-2″ measuring between the string nocks.

In both of the above cases a person will find that the angle which is formed by the bowstring while at full draw will be less severe on the fingers. At the same time the bow will draw with a noted smoothness not found with a shorter bow.

(3) For the number of strands which are safe to use for various weight bows, two very popular synthetic threads used for archery today are listed; they are Fortisan #333 and heat-stretched Dacron S or H-207. In either case the same number of strands will do, even though the Fortisan appears to be a slightly larger string when completed. The following data pertains to the Flemish, corded loop or spliced loop strings; secondly, to the endless type string. Use 9 strands of either thread mentioned for bows up to 30 pounds pull, 12 strands for bows to 40 pounds, 15 strands for bows to 50 pounds, 18 strands for bows to 60 pounds, 21 strands for bows to 70 pounds and 24 strands for bows up to 80 pounds.

If an endless string is to be made, increase any of the odd numbers by one strand only.

(4) The length of a bowstring is found in the following manner: (A) measure the length of the *bow along the back* from *nock* to *nock.* (Note: do not measure the bow's over-all length, as this will only lead to confusion.) (B) A proper string length is one which will brace a bow to the fistmele height recommended by its maker or a qualified person, (*see* "Fistmele"), and is not a length which has a consistent variation with all varied bow lengths. However, it will be found that average length bows may be properly braced with strings which measure approximately 3¼ to 3½″ shorter than the nock to nock length as found in step (A). (C) A finished net bow string's length is found by measuring the exact inside distance between the extreme end of one loop to the extreme end of the other.

Check-draw: Some archers, usually those who shoot the "Point of Aim" method, use a device called the "Check-draw." This is a small extension which projects slightly forward of the back of the bow with its extreme forward end dipped downwardly and slightly lower than the arrow rest, but directly forward and in line with the rest. The forward end of this extension supports a short piece from a flat rubber band by means of a thin slot, which when not depressed by the weight of the arrow shaft, will extend above the top of the arrow shaft about ⅛". When the arrow point is to complete full draw, the top end of the rubber band will be visible. If the archer allows his arrow to creep forward before the release, the rubber check-draw will be bent down and out of sight. In many cases the check draw is made to fasten onto the arrow rest as an actual part of the rest itself.

The importance of this should be easily understood from the preceeding, as consistent full draw is very important to consistent elevation on the target and the "check-draw" if used properly will assure consistency.

Chicago Round: This is one of two rounds shot internationally by target archers in mail match competition. (*See* "Olympic Bowman League, O.B.L.")

Chrysalled: The words chrysal and chrysalled are two of archery's own words. Their meanings have reference to either an arrow shaft or a bow which has been bent to its near-breaking point; thus causing a fracture of the wood fibers. In either case the arrow or the bow will not necessarily have to be broken into pieces. (A) In the case of an arrow, a chrysal may appear as a fine scratch or somewhat irregular line which may partially or completely encircle an arrow shaft. An arrow shaft which has unmistakable evidence of a chrysal should be considered dangerous and it is wise to destroy it. (B) In the case of a bow which is chrysalled there may appear a single fine line across the belly or it may have a great many of these lines appear all of a sudden. If the back of the bow still remains free of any chrysals, it is sometimes wise to have this bow worked down and a new facing applied to it before it "blows up" and hurts the person using it at the time. In many instances in bows and arrows which develop these faults it may be traced to wood which was not too well-seasoned before use.

Note: Make certain that what appears to be a chrysal is not

actually a crazed, or cracked, finish before working down a bow. Crazing of finish often happens with inferior synthetics or lacquers.

Classification of Eligibility for the N.F.A.A.: (1) Expert Bowman Class "A," scores from 299 on up, (2) Expert Bowman Class "B," scores from and including 229 to 298, (3) Bowman, 159 to and including 228, (4) Archer, 88 to and including 158, (5) Novice, 10 to and including 87.

Classification of Eligibility for the N.A.A. (revised 1957): Is as follows: (1) Gentlemen may not compete against ladies in a ladies' event. (2) Ladies may compete against the gentlemen in any of the gentlemen's events, although this has never been done. The ladies may not compete in the Junior or Intermediate boys' or girls' events. (3) Intermediate Boy: One who *has not* reached his eighteenth birthday before the close of the tournament in which he is competing. An Intermediate boy may compete against Gentlemen in any gentlemen's event and for awards in that event. An Intermediate boy may not compete against the Ladies or Intermediate girls. (4) Intermediate Girl: One who has not reached her eighteenth birthday prior to the close of the tournament in which she is competing. An intermediate girl *may* compete against ladies and intermediate boys in their respective events and for awards in those events, but this is seldom done in practice. (5) Junior Boy: One who has not reached his fifteeenth birthday at the close of the tournament in which he is competing. A Junior boy may compete against intermediate boys in their events and for awards in the events, but he may not compete against Junior and Intermediate girls in their events. (6) Junior Girl: One who has not reached her fifteenth birthday at the close of the tournament in which she is competing. A Junior girl may compete against Junior and Intermediate boys in any of their events and for awards in those events. (7) Beginner Boy: One who has not reached his twelfth birthday before the close of the tournament in which he is competing. He may not compete against the young ladies in any of their events. (8) Beginner Girl: One who has not reached her twelfth birthday before the close of the tournament in which she is competing. A Beginner girl may compete against Beginner boys in any of their events and for awards in those events. Such competition almost never takes place, however.

Classification, Clubs: In many larger local clubs the divisions for gentlemen, ladies, and children may be quite similar to those shown for the N.A.A.; small clubs usually have gentlemen, ladies, boys and girls with an age limit of 15 to 18 years for the intermediate division.

Clubs often have classes based upon the scores which are being shot by its members. The classes may read as follows: "AA" class 650 American round or over, "A" class 550 to 649; "B" class 450 to 549; "C" class 375 to 449, "D" class 300 to 374, and Novice class up to 300. (These scores are only as an example.)

Clout Shooting—(target archery): Clout is a fascinating target round which is enjoyed by gentlemen, ladies, and children.

A clout target for target archery is one which is laid out upon the ground in a true circle with white lines. The scoring rings must be in direct proportion with those of a standard 48″ target at the rates of one foot to each inch. The lines may be approximately two inches wide and must be of a substance which will not injure either the arrows or the archers.

The center of the target is usually indicated by a triangular or rectangular flag which is a bright color. This flag may be from 16 to 36 inches long and from 12 to 24 inches wide. The flag should be mounted on a round stake which will stand three to five feet above the ground.

A shooting line for target clout may not be more than fifty yards long and the rules which apply to target archery are used.

Because of irregularities of the ground and the variance in the line width, a wire should be attached to a round ring which is around the center flag stake. Upon this wire all necessary spacing must be accurately indicated. All spacings should be painted with the corresponding target colors. When in use the line is to be drawn tightly and rotated about the target circle as the value of each arrow is indicated.

An arrow which sticks into either the flag or the center stake shall be called a nine and all other valuations are equal to those of a standard 48″ target which are 9, 7, 5, 3, and 1. All questionable arrows shall be left unpulled until decided upon by the field officials.

It is customary for all archers to be given the opportunity to observe the locations of their arrows each end before any arrows are removed by the appointed arrow pullers. Each arrow puller must sort all arrows which have fallen into his respective ring and place them neatly together for rapid identification by their owners.

The scoring officials call the names of the archers in the order in which they are upon the scoring sheets. The archers may advance into the target to identify their arrows for their score at that time only and must leave the target immediately thereafter. *See* also, Rounds (target archery). Note: The position of the arrow point in the target determines its value.

Clout Shooting (field archery): (*See* "Battle Clout.")

Columbia Round (for ladies): The Columbia round constitutes the shooting of four ends or 24 arrows from each of the following distances: 50, 40, and 30 yards. A standard 48" target is used.

Commercial Equipment: This term, used in most cases, refers to factory or mass-produced tackle. Not necessarily of low grade, as many of the top Bowyers and manufacturers produce excellent products.

Composite Bow: A bow which is made from a combination of more than one specific material. Sometimes composite bows have a different material for each of its many parts. (*See* "Bow Types," step D.)

Compton Medal of Honor: This medal is awarded by the N.F.A.A. to archers who have served archery in an outstanding way for a period of years. This medal is in honor of W. J. "Chief"

The two sides of the W. J. "Chief" Compton Medal of Honor. This medal is of a gold colored metal, ¼" thick and 2½" in diameter. The hunting scene which shows the "Old Stump" and the deer is the same side of this medal which is used for the Compton Sportsman's Medal.

Compton who served archery in an outstanding way and yet he himself stood in the background and allowed others to "reap the harvest," so to speak. "Chief" Compton taught both Arthur Young and Dr. Saxton Pope how to shoot the bow and arrow.

Compton Sportsman's Medal: This medal is awarded by the N.F.A.A. to archers who have done something for archery beyond the realm of good sportsmanship. It is similar to the Compton Medal of Honor but is blank on one side.

Constitution, Club: The fundamental or organic law of a club which is framed by the early members of that, or a "mother" club with which it may be associated.

Conventional Bow: This type of bow is one which has its riser on the inside of the arc formed by the bow's limbs, when drawn or braced for shooting, and also a bow that the string centers down the entire length of its limbs and handle. Therefore, in case of this type of bow, unlike the "near or semi and completely centershot bows," the arrow must pass around the bow rather than alongside of it. (*See* "Paradox, Archers," and "Near or Semi and Completely Center Shot Bows.")

Conventional Bow Riser: One that is built with the riser on the belly or inside of the bow and may be of any of the "Bow types." (*See* Nomenclature Drawing.) (*See* "Non-conventional Bow Riser.")

Corded Loop: Has reference to the type of loops which are actually twisted into a rope-like manner as is the case of the Flemish type of bowstring. (*See* Nomenclature Drawing of the Bowstring.)

Creeping: To creep is to allow the arrow point to move forward of the back side of the bow slightly before the actual release. This habit should never be allowed to develop as it has these consequences: (A) Inconstancy in elevation on the target due to varied cast of the bow which is directly related to the length of the arrow. (B) Plucking the string, or jerky release, which is a result of trying to instantaneously pull the arrow back to full draw before the release; either of which is bound to "throw off" the aim. Creeping is usually termed "creeping on the draw." (*See* "Check-draw.")

Crest (of an arrow): The crest is the combination of colors on an arrow used to identify one set from another while shooting and scoring.

"Creeping on the draw." Have a fellow archer point out this fault before it becomes a habit.

Cresting Machine: A jigg which is used to simplify the painting of arrows. Some of these jiggs are merely a simple box with a support for the arrow nock separated by a space with another rest to support the shaft. With a jigg of this type the arrow must be rotated by hand. Other more elaborate cresting jiggs are motor driven with rubber chucks to support the nocks and padded rests to support the shaft while it is being rotated. These jiggs usually have adjustable pointers to designate the color spaces and their locations.

Crossbow: Modern crossbows are very handsomely made of wood and steel, etc., and are capable of extremely accurate shooting. The modern crossbow's draw weight seldom exceeds that of 150 pounds pull, usually considerably lighter, thus eliminating the need for a cocking device.

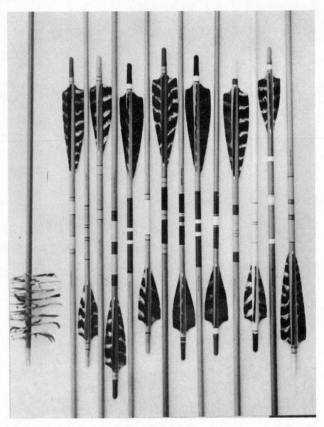

A few decorative arrow crests. The Flu-flu arrow has a solid color dip crest.

In N.A.A. competition all crossbows must be hand-drawn for cocking.

As to the rounds which are shot in the crossbow division, the Quadruple American Round, shot by ladies or gentlemen, is used to determine the National Champion. Other rounds are the Clout Round and the King's Round. (*See* "Arbalest," "Crossbow," and "Rounds, crossbow.")

Cross Hairs: Fine lines which are either painted or engraved by etching onto a sight lens or upon the reticule of a hunting optic. (*See* "Reticule," and "Sight, Bow.")

Curara or Curare: This is a deadly poison which is known to be and has been used by the Indians of South America where curare is presently used in medicine by skilled physicians as a shock treat-

A home made production cresting machine in operation. The operator is painting fine pin stripes between the crest colors.

ment and anesthetic prior to surgery. Its use is not suggested for hunting with bow and arrows. If this poison accidentally came into contact with the human blood stream by a wound, it might prove to be fatal. This poison acts upon the end plates of the motor nerves and allows the sensorial nerves to continue their functions until death, which is caused by paralysis of the respiratory organs.

It is true that the use of this poison is a humane way of killing game. An animal does not become violently ill but numbed as if sleep had overtaken it, but the element of human danger is not worth the risk which is involved. (*See* "Anti-coagulant.")

Custom Bows and/or Arrows: Those which are made to order, or usually of the higher degree of craftsmanship and materials. There is a very broad line between most custom bowyers and a beginner in this trade, but unfortunately many bowyers who are beginners at the trade like to use the words "custom made."

Dallin Medal: This medal is the championship Medal of the N.A.A. It is awarded in gold, silver and bronze to the top three contestants in the ladies' and men's divisions in the annual National Tournaments. A bronze Dallin Medal is awarded to girls and boys intermediate champion in each category. (*See* "Medals N.A.A.")

Deflexed Bows: A bow which is "Deflexed" is one which has a mid or handle section built into a pre-bent curve; the purpose of which is to add stability to the bow. The center of thrust of a "Deflexed" bow is usually behind the general line formed by the back of the bow's limbs; i.e., if a string is drawn from tip to tip on the belly side of a bow of this type, it is not uncommon that it will be somewhat above the inside of the handle riser, even though the bow would not be braced for shooting. (*See* "Bow Types," "Grip" and "Sighting Window.")

De-nocking an Arrow: To de-nock an arrow means to remove the string from the arrow nock while in the process of "the draw." This error in one's shooting is often a result of starting the draw while the index finger of the bow hand is still across the arrow shaft in a manner of holding it to the bow. The result will lead to considerable confusion as the arrow will fall to the ground when it is released and in many cases the forearm of the bow hand will be severely slapped by the bowstring. Other reasons for this error are nocks which are too loosely fitted to the bowstring, or nocks which are too tight to allow the string to be completely seated into the nocks.

One should never start the draw while the arrow is being held by the index finger of the bow hand. Always select arrows with nocks on them which will properly receive the necessary bow string size.

Density of Grain: In archery wood density plays an all-important part. It is common knowledge that a dense grained piece of stock has better elasticity than a soft punky piece of the same kind of wood. Aside from its elasticity, a piece of sound dense grained wood will withstand far more abuse and flexing than a soft open grained piece of stock.

Depth Perception: That quality of a picture or view which has depth beyond the actual subject being viewed; i.e., a picture or view which seems to have depth to infinity, or one which is not flat in appearance to the senses. Depth perception to an archer is that quality of the senses which enables him to intuitively perceive distance by observation. (*See* "Aiming Eye.")

Diana Bowl: Although this beautiful bowl remains in the custody of the N.F.A.A., the names of each year's National Ladies Champions are attached to its rim, engraved on a round silver disc. This bowl, fluted and very feminine in design, is made of sterling silver. It stands about eight inches high and is about twelve inches in diameter. This award was made possible by contributions from the archery tackle manufacturers, and is inscribed as follows: "The Diana Bowl, Women's Championship, National Field Archery Association. Gift of the Artillers, 1946." (*See* "Artillers.")

Dip Crest: A dip, or dipped crested arrow, is one which has been forced down into a tube or can filled with colored lacquer. A dip crest serves these purposes: (A) A protective covering to the arrow shaft and a good base onto which the feathers may be cemented. (B) A dip crest is also to identify one set of arrows from another which may have a painted crest. The dip crest may be either the latter portion, or the entire length of a shaft.

Dipping Arrows: The process of coating an arrow shaft with lacquer or other suitable protective coat, rather than to spray or to brush it onto the shafts.

Dipping Rack: A rack which is used to stand freshly dipped arrows onto. The rack trough returns the drained off finish into the dipping tube or container. A dipping rack is in a sense a production method of finishing arrows. The rack should never be subjected to a draft of air.

Dipping Tubes: Containers which have a length of pipe soldered to the bottom for added depth. A one-gallon can with a thirty-inch piece of two-inch galvanized down spout attached to the bottom of the can makes a fine dip tube. The hole through the can must be cut through to the tube and, of course, the bottom of the tube must be closed to completely eliminate leakage.

Divisions, Field Archery: (*See* "Field Archery Classifications").

Don'ts for Archery: (1) Never forget that the bow and arrow (target or otherwise), is a lethal weapon. (2) Never aim a bow and arrow in the direction of anything or anyone other than a target. (3) Never shoot, or draw your bow to shoot when a person is in front of the target. (4) Never shoot an arrow up into the air just to see how high it will go—it has to come down and you nor anyone else can say exactly where it may strike. (5) Always step back from the shooting line so that others may see who is still shooting. (6) Always inspect your bow, bowstring, and arrows before using them; any one or all may have danger signs of breaking soon. Neither a cracked bow, a slivered or chrysalled shaft, or a frayed bowstring should be considered safe—*they will not be.* It is a wise archer who will immediately replace a questionable string, deliberately break a fractured arrow, and unstring a weak bow. (7) Never shoot over a building or into a thicket. (8) Be *positive* that no archer is behind the target you plan to shoot at. (9) Always leave a bow standing in front of a target where there are archers looking for arrows. (10) Courtesy to your fellow archers creates good relations and better scores for all concerned. TO PRACTICE THE GOLDEN RULE ON AN ARCHERY RANGE OR IN THE FIELD SHOULD BE THE PRECEPT OF EVERY ARCHER.

Draw: To draw is to pull the bowstring as is necessary to shooting the bow and arrow. It is unwise to draw another person's bow without his consent to do so, and never without the proper length arrow for the bow. The draw is usually accomplished by drawing the bowstring with three fingers, one above the arrow and two below the arrow. The string is usually held at the first joint of the fingers or slightly nearer to the tips of the fingers for a smooth release of the string. The wrist of the string hand should be straight and in a manner which will align the back of the hand with the forearm. (*See* also "Fall Off.")

Draw Length: A person's draw length for the corner of the mouth (field draw), or the point of the chin (target draw), may be found by extending the arms and fingers completely "spread eagle" and take 38% of the total span measurement. Another method, not quite as satisfactory, is to hold a "yard stick" against the breast bone and extend both hands, fingers extended to full arm's length along side of the yard stick. The reach is measured at the ends of the finger tips. (*See* also "Charts and Formulas.")

Drift: The drift is caused by a cross and/or a quartering wind or breeze. The amount of drift in turn relates to the distance that an arrow is carried from its aimed path.*

---

* It has been observed that if the quartering wind is from the right to left, shooting arrows with right wing feathers will offset the amount of drift to a small degree, vice versa for a left to right quartering wind or breeze.

Dowel: The milled or turned shaft for an arrow, also a short piece of round shaft used to join pieces together.

Doweling Machine: A special piece of machinery which is used to mill square sticks into round shafts. For archery; to mill arrow shafts.

Eligibility Rules for Classification of the N.A.A.: (*See* "Classification, N.A.A.")

Emblems, Club: Most clubs adopt some sort of a club emblem symbolic of a local or historical landmark or myth. Either embroidered on cloth or printed for decals, emblems are an important asset as a club distinction and should be used whenever possible.

End: An end is a flight of arrows or a portion of any specific round. The number of arrows which may constitute an end may vary. In the United States an end in target archery is always six arrows at National tournaments shot "three and three"; in International tournaments an end is three arrows, while in a field round an end may constitute from one to four arrows, depending upon the target.

Endless String: An endless bowstring is one which when finished actually has two ends or loops, but is so called because of the manner in which this type of string is made. To make an endless string two pegs are spaced any given distance apart. The thread which is to be used is tied to one of these pegs and thence wound about the pegs until the proper number of strands is evident, at which time the two loose ends of the thread are tied together. The strands are then bound at the ends of the string, called the serving, and after the strands are served they are further bound together to form the string loops. The center section of the string should also be served or bound to eliminate wear which completes the "endless" string.

Eye: The end loop of a bow string.

Facing (bow): Laminations which are applied to the belly side of a bow. Facing may serve one or two purposes: (A) to increase a bow's draw weight, or (B) to increase the cast or acceleration. Materials used for this purpose are: (1) wood, (2) plastics, (3) laminated fiberglas.

Farewell Arrows: At the close of many large archery tourna-

These three emblems are typical of those which are adopted by archery groups and clubs throughout the world. They are necessary to the identification of an archer while shooting on courses or ranges other than his own. Emblems should be self-explanatory as to the locality of each club. The colors of the Desert Bow Hunters emblem, typical of those which are found on the desert lands, are a yellow background, brilliant orange sun, bleached white skull, light tan cactus and black lettering with black trim. The size is 4⅜". The Instinctors emblem has a background of bright green; the little skunk wears a hat of scarlet red while the lettering is also of red. The patch is white-trimmed with an outline of black. The emblem size is 4-15/16" over its extreme outer border of white. The emblem of the Tulare County Archery Club has a white embroidery background with a bright blue center, blue lettering and a black broadhead and bow. The size is 3".

ments each participant will shoot a farewell arrow which has his crest, name and complete address on the shaft. After all arrows have been shot, all of the archers proceed to the area where the many arrows have fallen. Each archer picks up one arrow and keeps it as a souvenir.

Fall Off: The most exasperating fault of a beginner is to have the arrow fall from the arrow rest while starting the draw of the arrow. This fault is due to excessive clenching of the arrow nock, or by

By reaching for the bowstring the back of the hand remains straight and lessens the danger of the arrow falling from the rest as the draw continues.

starting the draw with the bow held too near to the body. The latter allows the archer to start the draw with the wrist of the string hand in a crooked manner. As the bow tension will increase, the wrist of the string drawing hand will be straightened out by the string tension. This in turn will usually lift the arrow from the arrow rest into a falling off manner.

It must be remembered that while drawing an arrow the fingers which draw the string also hold the arrow nock onto the string. Thus, to clench the string with the fingers too tightly against the arrow nock will easily lift an arrow from the arrow rest if the elbow of the string hand is allowed to drop below the plane of the arrow shaft and the arrow rest, or if the wrist is allowed to straighten out after the draw is in motion.

To eliminate fall off, start the drawing of the arrow with the fingers which are to draw the arrow held only lightly against the nock of the arrow and with the bow arm as near to complete extension as possible—this in turn forces one to reach for the bowstring with the back of the wrist in a straight line with the forearm. In turn, one will find that the arrow will remain on the arrow rest completely through the draw, and until the release is completed.

Feathers (arrow): Also referred to as an arrow's fletching. Those which are preferred are from the large male Tom turkey, or other large birds. The wing tip feathers are preferred due to their extra body and stiffness. Because the natural oils have to be partially removed to dye a feather, the natural feathers are preferred as they will withstand more abuse and last longer. (*See* "Plastic Fletching" and "Vane.")

Feather Angle: The angle which the feather is applied to an arrow shaft. Note: A feather which is applied to an arrow shaft on an angle does not necessarily mean that it is applied with a true helixical spiral (*See* "Helix Spiral"). A left wing feather must be applied to an arrow shaft on an angle which places the back end of the feather nearest to the nock, to the right of the shaft center line and thence across the center line to the left side of the shaft center line while looking towards the arrow point; vice versa applies to a right wing feather. An arrow fletched with left wing feathers will rotate to the left while in flight.

Feathers (Base ground): Feathers whose quills are specially and precisely ground or cut to a uniform thickness and width which allows for exacting application to well made arrows. (*See* "Oil Line, feather.")

Feather (left wing): A left wing feather from the left wing of the bird has the base to the bottom side of the feather and while looking towards the front or quill pointed end, the bowed side of the feather will be on the left. One will notice that if the feather is a natural barred or striped feather the bright pattern will be on the left or convexed side.

Feather (right wing): The opposite of a left wing will have the base of the feather to the bottom side of the feather vanes while its bowed side will be on the right as you look towards the quill or pointed end. The brightest side of a right wing feather will be on the right side.

Feather Ending: This term is used more specifically to explain the process of tapering the strand ends of a Flemish type bow string before working the twist into the corded ends and while making the string loops. Any tapering must be done before any of the strands have been waxed with beeswax.

Feather Ending of Handle Riser: The mid section of composite laminated bows have an insert block shaped to give depth to the bow stave at its handle section and also a gentle dip into the bow limb. This insert is tapered to a paper or feather thickness at its two ends to allow for a smoothness in limb design. (*See* nomenclature drawing.)

Feathers (stripped): A stripped feather is one which has had its vanes pulled carefully from the base or quill. A stripped feather is not as easy to apply with preciseness to an arrow as one which has been base ground.

Feather Trimmer: A special die or electrically heated wire for the purpose of cutting or burning arrow feathers or the fletching of an arrow to the desired shape. The electric trimmer is by far the most popular method in use today. Most electric feather trimmers are home made; however, there are a few very fine models which can be obtained from archery dealers and suppliers.

Field Archery: The bow and arrow has been proven a modern hunting weapon and one requiring the greatest of skill, compara-

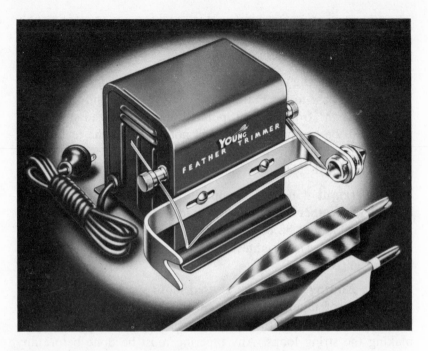

The modern method of trimming arrow feathers is by use of an electric trimmer. These two trimmers are Young Feather Trimmer, used by many of the professional tackle makers, and The Fleetwood Trimmer, which is used by many of the individuals who make their own arrows. (Two photos courtesy of R. C. Young and The Fleetwood Archery Co., respectively.)

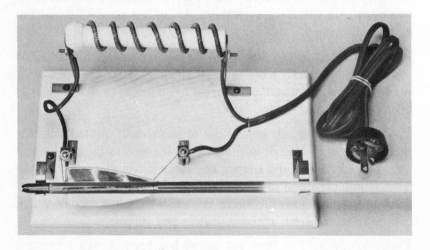

tively speaking. The sport has been divided into the following categories: (A) Tournament field shooting, which includes the use of various types of regular targets or animated targets of birds, animals or reptiles, etc. In tournament shooting each type of target will have a varied method of scoring value. (B) Field shooting, or roving as it is more commonly called, is actually the sport of going to the field and practicing by choosing targets such as logs, pine cones, stumps, tree trunks, bushes, etc., as the targets. In this type of practice usually enjoyed by two or more archers, the archer who scores the best on any chosen target will choose the next one. The distance to a target will vary from a few feet to 80 yards or more. (C) Hunting with bow and arrow is the pursuit of small and big game with the intention of actually killing and taking same, either as a sporting method, or for the necessity of food. Because of the popularity of bow hunting, most states now have regular archery game laws.

Field Archery Classifications: Field archers use two different methods of aiming and are divided into two separate divisions which are: (1) The first division is officially called the Instinctive division. This division is also referred to as "Bare bow," "Instinctors" and "Space aim Shooters," all having the same basic meaning; no bow sights on their bows, nor any calibrated markings of any kind attached to their bows which could be referred to as an aid to their aiming. (2) The Free Style division (pin shooters) which allows the use of various types of bow sights which may be calibrated and adjustable for all distances necessary to any type of field range. These two groups do not compete against each other in tournament competition since it has been proven that some archers who use sights have a very definite advantage over those who do not. In actual hunting it is usually to the advantage of the archer who shoots without the sight, especially if the target should be a running deer, etc.

Since the 1955 National Field Archery tournament the Bare Bow division has been subdivided to include a new and third group, known as the Hunters division. The first national competition in this group took place in the 1956 N.F.A.A. National tournament. The Hunters division operates as follows: These archers shoot the same rounds as the other two divisions; however, there is no classification within their ranks other than men, women, and juniors. The bare bow method of instinctive, or space aiming, must be used in this division and no sights or auxiliary aiming devices are allowed. The arrow weight must be based upon the following: (A) Men; a one ounce avoirdupois or 438 grains, based upon a 28-inch arrow. There is an adjustment of ten grains plus or minus for each one inch of arrow length; i.e., a 26" arrow must weigh 418 grains while a 29½" arrow must weight 453 grains. (B) Women and juniors; an arrow weight of 338 grains avoirdupois based upon a 28" arrow, with the adjustment of 8 grains per inch plus or minus; i.e., a 25-inch arrow must weigh no less than 314 grains, or a 27½ inch arrow must weigh no less than 334 grains, etc. (C) The length of the arrow shall be determined by the measurement from the bottom of the string nock to the shoulder of the point. (D) Any type of arrow material may be used for their construction; i.e., wood, dural, fiberglas, compressed wood, etc. (E) Archers of this division may compete in but one division only, and must make their preference known before entering a tournament.

Field Captain: In target archery, as well as field tournament shooting, the duties of the Field Captain are quite the same. First the field captain should be an archer who really knows the rules of whichever tournament he is to conduct. His authority and responsibilities are as follows: (1) to call the archers together for announcements, instructions, practice, and competition. (2) To direct, oversee and manage the competition and the conduct of all archers during that period. (3) To interpret and to enforce the club rules. The decision of the field captain is final and binding.

A field captain may appoint any assistants he feels are necessary to successfully and safely conduct the tournament, or he may request that this be done by the tournament committee.

Field Round, N.F.A.A.: (*See* "N.F.A.A. Rounds" and "Archery Ranges.")

Finger Tabs: A finger tab is used for the same purpose as a shooting glove; i.e., to protect the fingers while shooting the bow and arrow. There are several variations of shooting tabs. Most of these styles are made from select first quality horse hide, however there are a great many made of cowhide.

Finishes for the Bow: Many of the competitive lines are finished

Two versions of the finger tab more common to the archers of the past thirty years. (Photo courtesy of Warrior Manufacturing Co.)

Two views of an entirely different type of a tab which is fashioned similar to the shooting glove. This tab has the compactness of the regular tab. (Photo courtesy of King Sport-Line)

with fast drying lacquers or synthetics. The fine grades of custom made bows are usually finished with two or more coats of a fine grade of clear synthetic varnish or station wagon varnish. Either of these is superior to lacquers for a bow due to the flexibility necessary to withstand the constant bending of the bow limbs. Lacquer finishes are either sprayed or dipped onto a bow; whereas the varnish finishes are usually applied with a small sable bristled brush which requires considerable skill to do properly. It must be remembered that if the finish becomes crazed, moisture is sure to get into the bow which does not add to its cast, nor does it add to the appearance of a good bow to allow the finish to become shabby.

Finishes for Arrows: For all practicability the finish used for arrows will consist of a lacquer or cellulose base or a finish which when applied will allow the feather adhesives to adhere to it with a good sound bond. Arrow finishes may be clear or colored and are generally dipped for production work and also to save on materials. Note: Most adhesives used for arrow feathering are of a cellulose base and this type of adhesive will not adhere to an arrow finish containing varnish gums with any satisfaction.

Fishing Arrows: Arrows which are equipped with special points for the purpose of taking fish with bow and arrow. (*See* "Fishing, Bow and Arrow," and "Arrow Types.")

Fishing, Bow and Arrow: As a worthy pastime a great many archers have taken to the sport of bow and arrow fishing for Carp, Gar and other species of rough and unprotected fish.

The necessary equipment to fish with bow and arrow will consist of a bow, some regularly equipped fishing arrows, a spinning or free feeding type reel and about twenty to forty yards of tangle resistant line that tests 20 to 30 pounds, a row boat, canoe or flat bottom punt, a good fresh water stream or lake, and the fish. However, before going further here, a few comments in regard to the fish points, arrows, and the reel are necessary to supplement the pictures which accompany this outline. There are probably as many designs of fishing arrow heads as there are designs for broadheads, each having its good features and some their poor ones. The better of the fish heads comprise of the ferrule or head and a retractable or removable bard of some type in order for easy removal. Others which are less costly have stationary barbs which are fine to catch the fish with, but difficult to extract. The shafts most common to the fishing arrows are fiberglas (solid, not hollow), cedar, douglas fir, or Norway pine. The solid fiberglas shaft is very good as it needs no protective finish and is suitable for deep water shooting because of its weight. The wood arrows require a protective finish of a good grade of exterior or marine varnish which should be applied after the fletching. If a fish arrow is fletched with feathers, which is not absolutely essential, the vanes

Bernard (shooting) and Tony Jr. Novy fishing from a canoe on Monitowoo River, Manitowee, Wis. (Photo courtesy of Syd Herman)

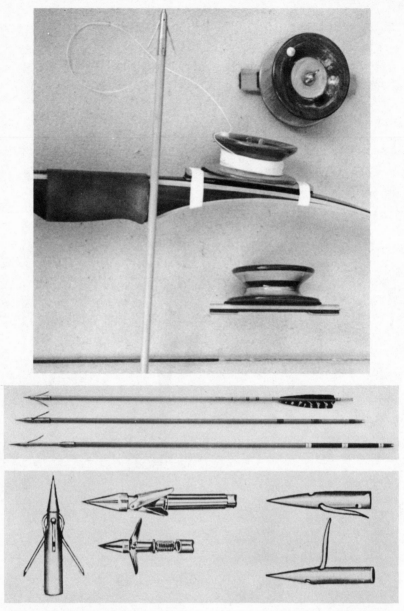

A few accessories necessary to fishing with bow and arrow. 1. A spinning type (above) of Bow reel ready for use (designed by author). 2. Three fishing arrows (center). The arrow at top (with feathers) has a Hill's fish head. The other two have Rota-Barb heads. 3. Left: (below)—The "Lee-Free" by S. C. Pierman; center top and bottom: a head by Parallel Plastics, Inc.; right side, top and bottom: "Rota-Barb" by Rolly Gottschalk.

must be coated with a protective waterproofing solution. If the vanes are rubber or plastic, no other precaution is required for them. The reel may be of any type capable of allowing the line to feed from it smoothly. The wind-up type of spinning reel is the fastest when retrieving the arrow, but the hand wound reels do a good job if the line is wound on them smoothly. The large reels shown in the pictures are very popular.

If fishing on the water rather than from the shore, the boat must be paddled very slowly until a swirl of fins appears, at which time all movements should stop until the fish are again feeding before any shooting takes place, then shoot a well aimed arrow into the midst of the fins. It is more often a hit than a miss under these conditions, but of course there are times when a single fish is the only target, so the answer to this problem is to take very careful aim and make a direct hit!

The method of attaching the line to the arrow is to drill a small hole immediately below the nock; thread the line from the reel through the hole and thence to the fish head. Another way is to attach the line to the head, draw it back along the shaft, and apply two or more half hitches to the back end of the arrow. The spin or free feeding reel is a must lest the line be shot into by the jerk of the arrow. If fishing for Gar or large river catfish, a gaff hook should be used if lawful in the area you fish; however, it should not ever be attached to the hand to be safe from drowning by being pulled overboard.

Should the fishing be done from the bank or a pier, the problem of refraction must be considered and requires considerable practice for success unless the fish are surface feeding. In any given depth of water the light rays to the fish are bent downwardly; therefore, one must aim to a point which appears to be short of the actual target. Otherwise, you will constantly overshoot the fish. The depth of the fish in the water will, of course, govern the refraction.

The food value of the Gar of North America is questionable. The common European Gar is a good food fish. As for the Carp, there are certain fresh water species which, if cooked by boiling or are smoked, are very edible. An article written for *True* Magazine, April issue of 1953, by Emmett Gowen, titled "I'll Take the Lowly Carp," will make your bow and arrow fishing even more pleasurable when you know what to fish for and how to prepare it after you have been successful.

Fistmele: This term is truly one of archery's own words and it means the distance to which a bow string should be spaced away from the back side of a braced bow. Depending upon the type of the bow, the fistmele will vary to some degree as some manufacturers request that their bows be braced to a maximum of 7½″ while others may say the fistmele may vary between 7½″ and 8½″, measuring from the back of the bow handle to the string. It is not proper to check this spacing by setting the first upon the inside of the handle with the thumb extended to its full length, as

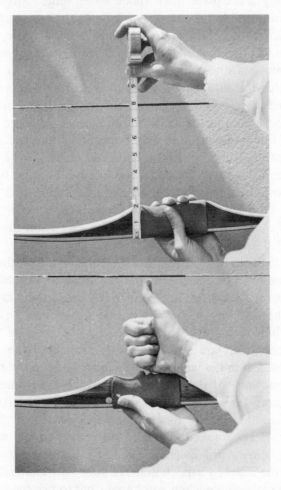

These two methods are used to measure the fistmele. The method using the ruler for accuracy is recommended.

many persons have larger hands than others which could mean that the string would be much higher than termed necessary.

Flat Bellied: A bow which is flat bellied is one which does not have a crown shaped belly as was popular with the English long bow design. The composite laminated bows are practically all absolutely flat bellied with only very slightly rounded edges. A thin flat bow will not pyramid in drawing weight but a short stacked type bow has a noticeable build up to the draw. (*See* "Stacked Type Bow.")

Flat Bow: A flat bow is one with a back and belly which are virtually parallel to one another (such as a slat or lath). The short flat bow was a modification of the long bow which was brought about by the American Indians. The flat bow has many designs, each of which is to lessen the "stack" of the drawing weight, and to increase the cast or acceleration without danger of breakage. Many of the flat bow designs are extremely short with wide thin limbs. The fact that a bow is of flat design does not necessarily mean, however, that it is limited to a straight limbed bow, as this is not at all the case. A flat bow may be of any shape or design. (*See* "Bow Types.")

Fletcher: A fletcher is one who fletches arrows; i.e., an arrow-maker.

Fletching: The applied vanes of an arrow. The fletching may be bird or turkey feathers or the fletching may be thin molded rubber vanes, or of molded plastic. The latter two are both available and have many good characteristics, but they also have a few "drawbacks." Weight is the main objection to rubber vanes, while fletching adhesives for plastic vanes are their main objection.

For many years the accepted number of feathers or vanes which were applied to an arrow has been limited to three; however, since 1956 there has been another great change. The vanes are shorter, lower, and from three to eight in number. The most popular quantity now seems to be four vanes set at either 90 or 75 and 105 degree angles, i.e., the 75 and 105 degree angle fletch means: (1) that as you would look at the nock end of an arrow with the nock slot in a vertical position, there are two vanes which are spaced at 37½ degrees in opposite directions to the vertical center line of the nock slot on both, the bottom and top sides of the arrow, therefore, (2) these vanes will be spaced 75 degrees apart at the bottom and top sides of the arrow, in turn, (3) the top and bottom vanes on either side of the nock slot will then be 105 degrees apart. As to the 90 degree fletch, the same example holds true excepting (1) that the top and bottom vanes are spaced at 45 degree angles in opposite directions to the vertical center line of the nock slot on both the top and bottom sides of the arrow, (2) in turn these vanes will be ninety degrees apart at the top and bottom sides of the arrow while, (3) the vanes on either side of the nock slot will also be 90 degrees apart. Note: Fletching jiggs which are made to fletch with the conventional three feather fletch require special adapters to be installed into the indexing units. These special fletching designs, other than the six feather fletch which would only require (that after applying three feathers to the arrow) that it be removed from the jigg and turned completely over on the indexing unit, and follow by adding another three feathers between those which are already there.

Either of these fletches have two vanes which pass along the side of the bow. Both types, having two feathers on the opposite side of the arrow which is away from the bow, have the advantage that these two feathers work as a buffer to the erratic side motions of the arrow as it passes the bow. The vanes being smaller eliminate drag resistance and allow for greater speed of the arrow, which in turn lends to a flatter trajectory from a lighter bow.

It appears that the objection to the 6 and 8 vane fletches is that in both cases one vane is positioned perpendicular to the nock in either direction, which would cause one of these vanes to pass next to the bow in either case. (*See* also Nomenclature of an Arrow.)

Fletching Cement: An adhesive used to cement the arrow vanes to the shaft. Cellulose based cements are most popular for feathers and Plio-Bond for plastic vanes.

Fletching Jiggs: A fletching jigg is one which is designed to hold the arrow shaft in a manner which will allow the vanes of the arrow to be attached to the shaft in their exact proper location. Some jiggs are designed to apply three feathers to the shaft simultaneously with either a degree of angle or a true helixical spiral. Other jiggs, usually preferred by professional arrow-makers, are designed to hold the shaft and allow for the application of only one feather or vane to be attached at a time. These jiggs are set up into batteries of twelve to sixty or more for each operator. The single vane jiggs are also manufactured to apply the vanes in a straight line, to a degree, or to a true helixical spiral with reference to the surface of the shaft.

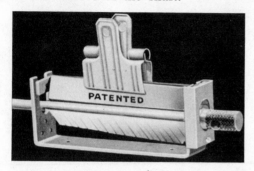

Fletching jiggs are quite necessary to all phases of archery. These jiggs are both very good models and are two of the many which are made for the trade today. The Spiro Fletcher (left) is for applying feathers to the shaft with a true helix spiral. (Photo courtesy of R. E. Rodes.) The Champion fletching jigg, with the angular base, is another of the many fine jiggs available to the trade. (Photo courtesy of The Lozon Archery Co.)

Fletching Pin: In some cases the vanes of the arrows are attached to the shaft by means of adhesives and are held in place by small sharp steel pins. These pins are thence called "fletching pins." To fletch with pins is an art easily learned and one worthwhile knowing as it gives the beginner something to do in his spare time without any additional expense of fletching jiggs.

Flight: In archery, target or field, flight shooting is shooting for distance. This type of shooting usually requires the very best of equipment to qualify. However, the fact that an archer has excellent flight-shooting equipment does not necessarily mean that he may win all of the events he may enter, as flight shooting requires perfect coordination and a great deal of practice to attain it.

Flight Arrows: Specially designed for distance shooting. These arrows usually are of boat-tailed or barrelled construction, with very short low-cut vanes, all of which are to eliminate resistance. Flight arrows require shafts made from extra select well-seasoned stock. Note: In many cases the author has made flight shafts from stock brought to him by experts in the flight business. The stock has been as follows: the back boards from an antique cabinet, the headboard of an early American bed, or a section of an old discarded telephone pole. In many cases these same archers may find one to five shafts out of a hundred or more which they would prize very highly.

Flight Bows: Any bow which is capable of shooting a good flight arrow to extremely long distances. Most flight bows are with recurved tip ends.

As an example of what is meant by extreme distances, a few of the records of the 1955 N.A.A. championship tournament are as follows: Larry Modlin, a Junior boy, shot 553 yards with a 50-pound bow; Cecil Modlin, Men's Unlimited Class, shot 614 yards, one foot; and Charles Pierson (Free style—foot bow) shot 774 yards. Both the first and the last of these set new world records. (For a complete list of all championship records through 1957, *See* "Records, N.A.A.")

Flight Bow Designation: Flight bows are designated as either hand bows or foot bows, according to the manner in which they are employed in a contest; i.e., a fifty-pound bow may be shot by holding it in the hand, or it may be classed as a foot bow and supported by a foot stirrup. However, foot bows are usually of very heavy drawing weights and a light bow would stand very little chance, comparatively speaking.

Flight Bow Weight Classes (N.A.A. 1957): The established weight classes are as follows:

(A) Men   50 lb., 65 lb., 80 lb., Unlimited, and Foot bows.*

(B) Ladies   35 lb., 50 lb., Unlimited, and Foot bows

(C) Juniors and Intermediates 35 lb., 50 lb., Unlimited, and Foot bows

Flinching: An archer who has gotten into the habit of flinching has considerable trouble doing as he plans to do, precision wise. This habit may be the result of nervousness brought on by hitting the bow arm with the string, sore fingers, tiredness, being under pressure score wise, trying too hard to do the impossible, or trying to see where the arrow is going before it is safe to drop the bow hand. The corrections for these faults in the same order are as

---

* Foot bows are also referred to as "free style" class.

follows: (1) One should wear an armguard and strive to hold the bow arm freely clear from the path of the bowstring. (*See* "Bow Hand Grip," part (1) and the Note: part (2).) (2) Never shoot a bow without the aid of a protective finger guard, tab or glove, for any period of time as sore fingers are very conducive to a poor release and flinching. (3) One should not shoot a bow which is too heavy, for to be relaxed while shooting is a paramount factor of good archery form and better shooting technique. A light weight fast bow, properly handled, will make as good a score, or better than a heavier bow poorly shot. Do not shoot until too tired to relax. This takes the enjoyment out of the game! (4) Forget your score and shoot for the enjoyment of the game. By doing so, your precision shooting will be easier to accomplish and less nerve-wracking. A tired archer does more flinching than he may realize, as he continually wonders if his tiredness is showing up on each arrow he (or she) happens to be shooting. (5) When a person tries too hard he is likely to do many things unconsciously. Again at this point it must be remembered that to be relaxed and free of any self-inflicted mental pressure is to insure yourself against the habit of flinching.

Flu-Flu Arrows: This arrow is one which is used for bird shooting or any shot at fairly close range. A flu-flu arrow is one which has a feather spiraled around the shaft in a corkscrew manner. Arrows of this type have very short range due to the resistance of the feather vanes which are seldom trimmed after they are applied to the shaft.

Following the String: A bow which "follows the string" is one which does not return to its original shape when unstrung after shooting. To follow the string does not necessarily mean that a bow lacks good shooting qualities as most good self bows will take a slight set in this manner and still shoot very smooth and fast. This is caused by cell compression on the belly side of a self bow and the elongation of the wood fibres on the back of the bow. Composite bows of comparatively recent design, which are faced and backed with good grades of fiberglas, seldom, if ever, follow the string due to the extremely low compression and/or stretching qualities of fiberglas backings and facings.

Foot Bow: These bows are usually of extremely heavy drawing weights which are shot by an archer from a lying down position. The bow is held onto the soles of the feet by means of a special stirrup and is drawn with one or both hands before the release. These bows are considered dangerous for one who is not acquainted with them or their proper use. A broken bow or string may result in a badly sprained or broken back, as well as other injuries.

Footings (arrow): A footed arrow is one which has a hardwood piece of stock inlaid into or onto its front end. A footing increases a shaft's weight and its spine or stiffness. A footing will increase an arrow's durability to a great degree, and with little danger of breaking off an arrow point. Another type of footed arrow is the compressed footing which is accomplished by using an arrow square which is larger at the front end than the back end. In turn the entire square is compressed to equal size for its entire length before it is doweled into a shaft. Shafts of this type are patented by William E. Sweetland of Eugene, Oregon, and are sold under the name of Forgewood* arrows.

Follow Through: This term means to retain the same correct stance and posture after the arrow is released that was evident before the release. The follow through, properly executed, should be held until the arrow hits the target. (*See* also, "Flinching").

Forgewood: Compressed cedar arrow shafts. These shafts are sold under two trade names, Forgewood* and Battleshafts.

Free Style Archer: An archer who may aim with either a regular bowsight or by means of marks across the belly side of the bow.

Free Style Flight: Shooting with a foot bow, or a bow which is attached to the feet by means of a stirrup. (*See* also "Flight Bow Designation.")

Full Draw: An archer's full draw is complete and proper when a correct length arrow is drawn to its point and the string hand is firmly anchored against the face prior to the release. Full draw is important each time as it assures the archer that the same thrust will be exerted from the bow every time.

Games, Archery: All of the following games or rounds which are listed are found under the headings given and are explained

---

* Registered trade mark of Wm. E. Sweetland, Eugene, Oregon.

A "full draw" with a high cheek anchor. Note the continued straight line formed by the arrow and the right forearm.

therewith: (1) Target archery games or rounds: (a) American Round, (b) American Round, Junior, (c) Clout, Ladies, Men and Juniors, (*See* "Rounds, Target Archery"), (d) Columbia Round, (e) Flight (*See* "Flight Bows," "Flight Bow Designations," "Flight Bow Weight Classes (N.A.A. 1957)," "Records, N.A.A.," and "Free Style Flight," (f) Hereford Round, (g) Indoor American Round, (h) International Rounds and International Rounds (revised), (i) Mail Match, (j) Metropolitan

Round, (k) National Round, (l) Olympic and Chicago Rounds (*See* Olympic Bowman League, O.B.L.), (m) Team Rounds, (n) Wand Shooting, (o) York Round, American and English. Note: In addition to shooting many U. S. rounds, the Canadians have a round of their own known as the Canadian Round; it is explained under that heading. (2) The Field Archery rounds are as follows: (a) The N.F.A.A. Field Round, (b) The N.F.A.A. Broadhead Round, (c) The N.F.A.A. Big Game Round, (d) The N.F.A.A. Hunter's Round, all of which are explained under the entry "N.F.A.A. Rounds," and under separate headings there are (e) Battle Clout, (f) Broadhead Flight, (g) Novelty Rounds. (3) The games or rounds shot in the Cross bow division are: (a) The Quadruple American Round, (b) The King's Round, (c) Clout Round, (d) Flight, (e) and Novelty Rounds. The latter three in accordance to committee rulings pending on the shoot date.

"Game Framer": A hunting optic which is made specifically for

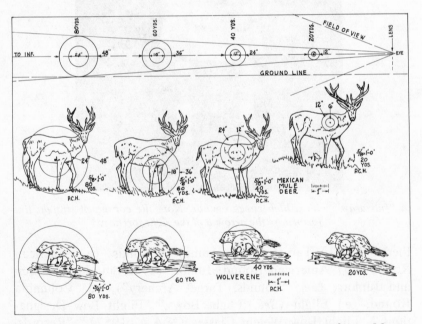

Fig. 13.—How to make use of this hunting optic. A Binocular or Monocular is helpful to a hunter, but when it is further supplemented by a means of distance calculation by association, it is more valuable. This does not infer that this optic removes all question of distance, but its use will be more accurate than a guess. The approximate size of the hunted game should be known.

use of hunting archers. The "Game Framer" incorporates within its field of view two circles, one within the other, and both with a common center. The outer circle will subtend exactly 6″ to each ten yards from "0" yards to infinity. To further explain this, the outer circle will be 6″ at 10 yards, 12″ at 20 yards, 30″ at 50 yards, 60″ at 100 yards, etc. The inner circle of this optic is made to subtend exactly one half the size of the outer circle, or 3″ to every 10 yards from "0" to infinity; i.e., the inner circle will be 6″ at 20 yards, 12″ at 40 yards, 18″ at 60 yards, 30″ at 100 yards, etc.

Example: Assuming that a person is viewing a Mexican Mule-tail deer from a distance where the outer circle will completely circumscribe the deer with the outer circle lowered to the position of the hoofs. It will take an approximate 60″ circle to do this; therefore, the distance would be merely 100 yards as the outer circle will increase or decrease 6″ to every 10 yards, or, 10 units of 6″ to each 10 yards = 60″ circle. The same method of calculation would be true if the inner circle would circumscribe this animal, necessitating a 60″ circle. However, if that be the case, the distance would be 200 yards, as $60″ \div 3″ = 20$ units of 3″ to each 10 yards, or $20 \times 10 = 200$ yards.

Since the above is strictly a mathematical example, and requires that the approximate size of the hunted game be known, it may sound confusing, but the archers who are using this optic have overcome this confusion by using it strictly in a manner of circle-size association and not in terms of feet, inches, or yards. By doing so it is just as easy as instinctively being able to view a target from sixty yards and estimate the distance by the elements involved—and the fact that hunting requires a good optic, the added convenience through practice is worth the effort.

Being a brand new type of optic, it is still in experimental use but available in either the 7×35 Monocular or Binocular with coated lenses.

Gear, Archery: Equipment in general: bows, arrows, armguards, gloves, tackle boxes, quivers, etc.

Glass Powered: A term used to identify a bow which is either all glass fibres, or one which is faced and backed with fiberglas.

Glove: (See "Shooting Glove.")

Glue: (*See* "Adhesives.")

Grading shafts: The selection of arrow shafts as to their degree of quality. The top grades of arrows require many steps in the grading of the shafts before they are finally ready to be made into a set of arrows. This accounts for the difference in prices of raw materials and matched arrow shafts in sets. A few of these steps to consider are: (1) soundness of grain, (2) straightness of grain, (3) straightness of shafts, (4) weighing, (5) spine testing, (6) matching into sets and, (7) matching the balance points if required.

Gravity and its Relation to Trajectory: While shooting a bow or any other propellent the downward force of gravity has a very important bearing upon the path of the projectile and its trajectory from the source of stored or kinetic energy to the target.

Without the force of gravity all projectiles would travel in an absolute straight path from the source of energy to the target, and if the target should be missed the projectile would continue on in the same straight line until its energy was used up completely and, at this point, it would remain; but this is not the case at all. In archery, the trajectory path of an arrow must be considered because there is a downward force or pull of gravity on the arrow, as well as on all things moving, moveable and/or immoveable, and because of this force all projectiles do travel in a curved arc from their source of energy, other than things which are set into absolute vertical motion (either straight up, or straight down), in which case the path will be a straight line, up or down.

A. In regular target archery arrows are shot over a comparatively level field. Therefore, as a hypothetical example, since all forces of gravitation are toward the center of the earth, and the fact that these forces extend *vertically* from all points of the earth's surface into the atmosphere, an arrow passing on a horizontal or level plane to the earth's surface for any given distance will be affected by a greater amount of the *imaginary* vertical lines of downward forces of gravitation than an arrow which may be shot either on a downward or an upward angle for that same distance.

B. With the foregoing in mind, in terms of hunting or field shooting, remember that shooting either downhill or uphill, an arrow will pass through fewer *imaginary* vertical lines of the downward forces of gravity than for the same distance shot on the level or horizontal plane; if you pull your arrow up to a complete full draw for a shot in either case and do not creep on the draw before the release, it is reasonable to assume that your arrow will travel on a flatter trajectory either on an angle of depression or elevation; therefore, if not compensated for by shooting a slight amount lower than on the level plane, you will over shoot your target.

Summary: Since the cast of a bow, the resistance of the arrow, and the angle of elevation or depression all have a bearing on the foregoing, one should do considerable practice on uphill and downhill shooting from varied distances to become familiar with the forces of gravitation in relation to the flight and trajectory of his arrow. (*See* "Trajectory.")

Greenhorn: A novice archer, a beginner. Perhaps this expression should be completely forgotten as it has many times been the reason for ill feelings, or self-consciousness, either of which is not conducive to good sportsmanship.

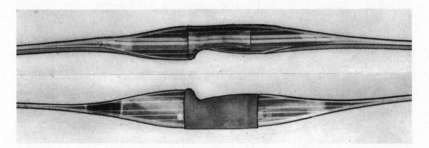

These two bows, although of the same type, appear to be completely different since one has a suede leather grip, while the other is finished and polished to glass smoothness.

Grip: The grip of a bow is the handle section where it is grasped for or while shooting. Some archers prefer the grip to be covered with leather with a suede roughened surface to prevent slipping in the hand, while others prefer that the handle space be sanded and finished to a glass smoothness in order that it may easily slip or rotate in the hand for alignment to the anchor point. To further aid a bow grip of the latter type to turn in the hand, many archers use talcum powder on the grip to add to its smoothness, which seems to have the action of a bow with its limbs inserted into ball-bearing sockets. It takes but a very slight twisting of a bow's grip to throw an arrow off of its aimed path; therefore, one should try both types of grips to find which type suits him the better. (*See* "Handle Types.")

Ground Quiver: (*See* "Quiver.")

Handicap System: In archery as in many other sports there are many lines of thought as to what constitutes a fair method of handicap and tournament participation; therefore, since both the National Archery Association and the National Field Archery Association have sound rules on handicapping aside from their many classifications, a request to either association for their most recent rulings would be sensible and in order.

Handle Riser: The mid-section of a bow where the bow is held while in use. (*See* Bow nomenclature drawing, "Grip" and "Handle Types.")

Handle Riser Insert: (*See* "Riser Insert.")

Handle Types: (1) First is the conventional straight handle with rounded corners to allow for ease and comfort while holding the bow. (2) A bellied handle has sides which are convexed or expanded to increase the size to the individual's hand. (3 a) The saddle type may have bellied sides or not, but in either case there is a definite dip into the upper end on the inside of the handle which allows the bow to seat to the hand more comfortably. The saddle type handle allows for even distribution of pressure to one's hand while shooting. (3 b) The most recent change in a handle design is that of a short Pistol grip fashioned on the inside of the bow handle which allows the archer to hold his bow as explained in part (3) of "bow hand grip," but with the fingers closed around the under side of the grip rather than along side of a conventional handle. (4) The center-shot handle may be of any of the preceding types. It is a handle which in most cases is slightly off-centered to the true centerline of the bow on the upper end which allows the arrow to pass near to or at the exact center of the bow. In the case of a conventional bow, the arrow passes around the side of the bow as the handle is centered equally to each side of the centerline. (5) A take-down handle is one which incorporates a steel or suitable metal ferrule as a joining mid-section to a bow as a joint in a fishing rod. A take-down handle is shaped to have the same appearance as a regular handle would have. This type of handle allows a bow to be taken apart, thus the bow would be only one half of its total length when ready to shoot. Dismantled, a take-down bow is very easy to carry, especially in brushy areas or in a car. They are easily stored due to the small amount of space required. Note: Further explanations of handle types may be found under the headings of "Conventional Bow," "Near or Semi and Completely Center Shot Bows," "Bow Types," Note (2) part (B), and "Sighting Windows." (*See* "Grip.")

Hanging Arrow: One which hits a target but does not penetrate deeply enough to stand at the proper angle to the target face. In target archery, the archer to whom a hanging arrow belongs may request that his shooting mates stop shooting immediately while the arrow is inserted into the target at the proper angle but only into the scoring area from which it was hanging. If this request is not made and the arrow falls from the target, the arrow would be placed in the red ring and the value would be a seven, even though the arrow may have fallen from the white or one ring of the target.

A hanging arrow is in a very dangerous place and may be shot into two pieces. Therefore it isn't often that an archer will allow it to hang on the target.

Heat Box: A box, usually thermostatically controlled, which is used to force dry adhesives and finishing materials.

Helix Blade Spiral: Some hunting blades or heads are made with a true helixical spiral. Blades of this design are exceptionally rigid; however, they require special attention to the fletching. A blade which would have a left spiral must also be fletched with left spiral; otherwise, the arrow will float or plane rather than spin while in flight.

Helix Feather Spiral: Arrows which are fletched with a true helixical spiral are those which have the fletchings, or vanes, not only at an angle to the concentric center line of the shaft, but the vanes also set at a right angle to the surface of the shaft at all points of contact.

Hereford Round (for ladies): Shoot twelve ends or 72 arrows from 80 yards, eight ends or 48 arrows from 60 yards, and four ends or 24 arrows from 40 yards.

Holding: The necessary time which it takes a person to aim an arrow properly before the release. Good shooting form constitutes the continuation of retaining the same stance after the release, which was apparent before the release, with this exception, —only the fingers of the bow hand should be in an extended position. Holding properly will eliminate flinching.

Horn Nocks: Decorative bow tips into which the string nock has been fashioned. This type of nock has not been popular since the early part of 1940 due to the ease with which they were broken from a bow. A very light jar would put an archer out of a tournament due to the loss or loosening of a horn nock. This type of nock has given way to the self nock which is an integral part of the bow. (*See* "Nocks, Replaceable Bow.")

Hunter's Division: A new division of the N.F.A.A. since 1955. The Bare Bow or Instinctive archers comprise this group and all must use equipment designated as heavy or hunting equipment. (*See* "Field Archery Classifications.")

Hunter's Round, N.F.A.A.: (*See* N.F.A.A. Rounds and Ranges")

Hunting, Archery: After one has had a reasonable amount of field and range practice a hunting trip to the field may be in order. Hunting with a bow and arrow does not necessarily mean all big game. There are small game targets such as squirrels, snakes, rodents, rabbits, birds, etc. These make good targets and will sharpen one's wits for the real big game.

For the more evasive big game an archer is wise to carry a Monocular or Binocular. The best within reasonable means is none too good. There is nothing quite so disturbing as to spot a deer early in the morning or at dusk and then be unable to see if it is legal game. The same applies to all game.

Do not make a practice of shooting at everything which moves. Be safely sure of your target. It may be another archer.

On your hunting bow the use of a jersey bow sox will kill all reflections and will protect your bow from scratches also.

Wear neutral or camouflaged colored clothing so that they will blend into the surroundings. Move slowly and always into the wind or air currents if at all possible. Animals have a keen sense of smell and can pick up a scent much quicker than they can see a hunter if he moves carefully. Do not smoke unless you are going to move on up wind before hunting again thereafter. Never smoke unless in a safe place and be sure that the cigarette is completely out before it is discarded.

For a person who would like to read some excellent books on hunting and hunting techniques the four listed here are worthwhile. *The American Deer Hunter, Small Game Hunting, Advanced Hunting on Deer and Elk Trails,* all three by Francis E. Sell, and *How to Hunt American Game* by Robert B. Vale. Of course, there are other good books on the subject of hunting but these four are outstanding for the use of a bow hunter, as well as a gun hunter. (*See* "Lure Calls" and "Lure Scents.")

Hunting Bow: Any good bow capable of shooting a legal hunting arrow with enough force to kill game at a distance of forty to one hundred yards. Some states have very rigid restrictions on hunting arrows and bow weights, however; therefore, the game laws in the locale in which a person wishes to hunt should be well checked before a law is unknowingly broken.

Impregnated Wood: A thin lamination or slat of fine grained hard wood which has been impregnated with phenol or another similar plastic. This type of wood is quite popular as bow facings and backings.

Index Nock: An arrow nock (self, reinforced or plastic replaceable) which has a small bump or rib which is perpendicular to the string slot. This index is on one side only and should be placed directly behind the cock feather of an arrow. The purpose of the index is to quickly identify the position of the cock feather and the position of the nock slot without the necessity of having to look at them. With an index nock, this can be easily done.

Indoor American Round: Many variations have been shot by the author, each having a different size target and each group having varied ideas as to the distances which should be standard, but— there is no such round. That is to say, there is no dwarf American Round for indoor shooting on short ranges. A true Indoor American Round is exactly the same as the regular American Round and requires the same distances and the regular 48″ target.

Instinctive or Space Aiming: Instinctive aiming is supposedly one's ability to aim and shoot a bow and arrow strictly by one's

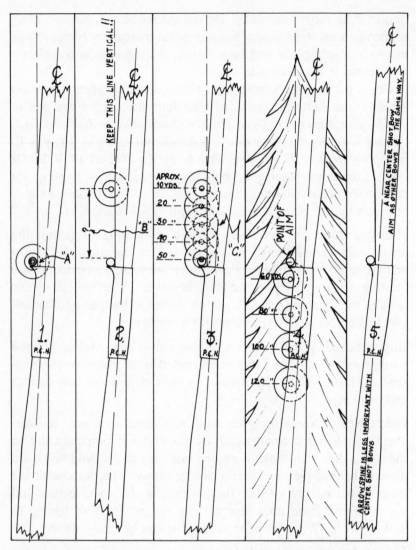

Fig. 14.—Instinctive, or Space Aiming: *Complete information is contained in this entry.*

instinct; i.e., to place the bowhand to the proper height, draw the arrow, aim without any means of aiming assistance, properly lead a running target, shoot in total darkness when nothing can be seen but the target, and—hit the target. There are things to be considered, however, before one is able to do these things as second nature, and are hereby covered as a series of questions and answers: (1) Does he leave both of his eyes open?—Only if he draws under or near to his master-eye, or if he can shoot better with both eyes open! (*See* "Aiming a bow and arrow," and "Aiming eye.") (2) How does one know how and where to start with this type of aiming, when he has absolutely no idea how to aim a bow and arrow without the aid of a bowsight?—By leaning temporarily on the "Space Aiming" method which is included under this heading until he has gained enough confidence and knowledge of shooting that he can gradually improve his ability to shoot without the "Space Aiming" thought in mind. (3) How does one learn to lead a moving target properly, and hit it?—By learning how to plan out his triangulation (*See* "Triangulation") to the target instantaneously and then to become adept at including this ability together smoothly and flawlessly with all of the other necessary points of good shooting form. (4) How does one shoot in absolute total darkness, when only the target face is illuminated?—He does not do so proficiently unless he can actually see the position of his bow hand in relation to his target which is technically "space aiming," the location of the hand in relation to the target. To further clarify the preceding, think seriously of this question—how well does one score when he is hoodwinked? One either has to see his target and his hand in relation to the target or he does not fare so well! (5) Does an instinctive archer see the space between his full drawn arrow and the bull's-eye before his release?—It is quite evident that whether he realizes it or not, he does; otherwise he would not return his hand to the same position, or to another, if correction was necessary. (6) Is a person born with the instinctive ability to do anything? Medical science says no. A doctor even has to slap a newly-born baby to get it to start breathing. Therefore, by facing these facts it should be granted that "Instinctive" and "Space Aiming" are closely united and that is the basic reason they are entered under this heading as such.

Instinctor: An archer who shoots his bow and arrows without the aid of any type of sighting device as further explained in "Instinctive or Space Aiming." These archers are presently of the "bare bow" classification in the N.F.A.A. and are called "Instinctors." The arm patch and identification emblem of this division of archers is unique since it has the animated figure of a very happy little skunk shooting a bow and arrow. (*See* "Emblems, Club.")

International Rounds: Prior to 1956 the following rounds were sanctioned by the Federation Internationale De Tir A L'Arc (FITA), which were to be shot in international competition for the titles "Champion" and "Championess" of the world. They were:

> 60 arrows from 70 metres or 76.6 yards approximately.
>
> 48 arrows from 60 metres or 65.6 yards approximately.
>
> 36 arrows from 50 metres or 54.7 yards approximately.

The International Long Round (for men):

> 72 arrows from 90 metres or 98.4 yards approximately.
>
> 48 arrows from 70 metres or 76.6 yards approximately.
>
> 24 arrows from 50 metres or 54.7 yards approximately.

The International Short Round which follows was shot by both men and ladies:

> 30 arrows from 50 metres or 54.7 yards approximately.
>
> 30 arrows from 35 metres or 38.3 yards approximately.
>
> 30 arrows from 25 metres or 27.3 yards approximately.

The 1955 International Championship consisted of a double Long Round and a double Short Round for both men and ladies. The longer distances of the Long Rounds (i.e., 90, 70, 60 and 50 meters) were shot on a standard 48″ target face of standard colors with each color divided into two equal parts by use of a thin line. However, values counted only 9, 7, 5, 3, and 1. The Short Round was considerably different. From 50 meters a standard 48″ face was used; however, each of the colored zones was divided into two equal parts by an additional fine black or white line. Thus, in every case for international competition, there were ten scoring spaces instead of five. The values of each were from center outward 10, 9, 8, 7, 6, 5, 4, 3, 2, and 1. (The higher value count was used only for the Short Round.) Therefore, the gold was 10 and 9; the red was 8 and 7; the blue 6 and 5; the black 4 and 3, and the white was 2 and 1. At 35 meters the faces were changed to one which was 0.80 meters, or 31.496″. This face was of the standard colors and proportionately the same spacings as the standard 48″ target face. This face was also divided into ten spaces, with the same values indicated. Now again at 25 meters a still smaller target face of 0.60 metres or 23.6″ was used. This face was also divided and valued as outlined. Note: 1 metre = 39.37 inches.

Although the Short Round somewhat resembles the distances and number of arrows shot in an American Round, the round is more difficult in that the target becomes smaller for each of the shorter distances.

International Rounds (revised): As of 1955 the delegates of FITA voted and passed, with vigorous protests by members from the United States and some other countries, to do away with the old rounds and henceforth use the following rounds for International competition. (To be called the FITA Round.)

For the ladies:

36 arrows from 70 metres or 76.6 yards approximately.
36 arrows from 60 metres or 65.6 yards approximately.
36 arrows from 50 metres or 54.7 yards approximately.
36 arrows from 30 metres or 32.9 yards approximately.

For the men:

36 arrows from 90 metres or 98.4 yards approximately.
36 arrows from 70 metres or 76.6 yards approximately.
36 arrows from 50 metres or 54.7 yards approximately.
36 arrows from 30 metres or 32.9 yards approximately.

Two of these rounds will comprise the championship, and in both cases the target will consist of the large standard 48″ target face from 90, 70, and 60 metres only, and the smaller .80 metre face (31:496″), will be used for the distances of 50 and 30 metres. In all cases, for *both large and small faces,* the values of the rings from the center out are 10, 9, 8, 7, 6, 5, 4, 3, 2, and 1. In the International Championship tournaments a point of aim may be used and, as of 1956, a simple pin type sight may be used. No types of lens or prisms may be used. A "kisser" is allowed if small. (*See* "Kisser.")

Jar: A bow which does not have a smooth action following the release is one which has a jar. Common reasons for bows with this quality are heavy tips and/or limbs bending too near to the handle section.

Kick: Relates to a bow's lack of smooth shooting qualities. A bow which has a kick is one which is rough and uncomfortable to shoot.

Kiln Dried: A method of force drying woods in an oven, usually specifically for this purpose. The fact that a piece of bow or arrow stock has been properly kiln dried rather than naturally air seasoned does not mean that it is not a good choice. If properly handled, kiln dried stock is capable of rendering both fine bows and arrows.

King's Round: (*See* "Rounds, Crossbow.")

Kisser: A bowstring "kisser" is a small bump added to a bowstring which is placed at the exact position where the bowstring meets the archer's lips when using an under the chin anchor point.

Kissing the String: Archers who draw to the center of the face and under the chin (low target archery anchor point) often touch the drawn bowstring with their lips. This is done as a check on whether or not they have completed the draw. If not, they will be unable to feel the string against their lips. Thus the expression "kissing the string."

Knurler: A device used to crimp an arrow point in a manner which will lock it, so to speak, onto the forward end of the arrow shaft. Arrow points which have been knurled onto an arrow often necessitate heating considerably over an open flame in order that they may be removed for replacement.

Lady Paramount: A field captain in the ladies' division of an archery tournament. The duties of a Lady Paramount are the same as the Field Captain in the gentlemen's division. (*See* "Field Captain.") The Lady Paramount is appointed by a tournament committee. She may appoint any assisting officers she deems necessary to her duties or she may request that these assistants be appointed also by the tournament committee.

Let Down: Refers to loss of cast or acceleration, or drawing weight. Either of these may be directly a result of being overheated by the sun's rays, or by a period of long usage. The modern composite type bows which are faced and backed with fiberglas are practically devoid of this fault due to the extreme low percentage of compression and/or stretch of glass fibers from which the backings and facings are made.

Locked Elbow: An archer who keeps the elbow joint in a vertical rigid position as he shoots uses the "locked elbow." This form is preferred by most archers as it aids in consistent length of draw and tends to keep the arm from the path of the bowstring. (*See* "Bow Hand Grip" Part (2) Note.)

Long Bow: This definition is legally given to all archery bows other than those which are attached to the stock of a cross bow or an arbalest. There are many kinds of long bows, all of which may be found under the heading of "bow types." The basic difference in long bows of earlier years in comparison to those of recent years is the deep, narrow limb cross section of the English long bow and the thin, wide flat cross section of the modern bows; but, technically either type is a long bow. The use of the long bow has been traced back for many centuries as a defensive weapon and as a means of food supply. In recent years the long bow has been used basically for play; however, even more recently the taking of game with bow and arrow has gained tremendous popularity and commands considerable respect as a truly sporting weapon.

Loops, String: The loops of a bowstring are the ends of the string (*See* Bowstring nomenclature).

Loose: This term refers to the actual release of the bowstring from the fingers or the drawing aid, or to put an arrow into motion by releasing the string.

Lure Calls: An increasing number of hunters of both the gunmen and archers are now using hunting lures. These gadgets, to name a few, represent the squall of a wounded rabbit, the bleat of a lamb, the caw of a crow, the chirp of a squirrel. The purpose of the lure calls is, of course, to attract the attention of the particular kind of game which is being hunted; i.e., a rabbit call lure to attract a predatory animal such as a fox, coyote, bobcat, etc., or a crow call to attract the attention of a crow, and to entice them into shooting range. The use of some types of lure calls has opened a new thrill to the bow hunting field, and a great many archers have succeeded in becoming very successful through their usage. Of course lure calls are not new to the human race because the Indians depended a great deal upon stalking their game with them.

Lure Scents: Aside from lure calls, another type of lure which is regaining popularity with trappers, bow and arrow and gun hunters, is the scent-type lure. Some types of scent lures are used to bait traps and are formulated to attract game to the trap, while others are formulated to kill the human body scent which enables the hunter to approach his game undetected, whether the stalk is from down wind, up wind, cross or quartering wind. This latter lure type was used by the Indians and early day hunters who depended upon kills from short ranges. Examples of these latter lures are those formulated from the scent glands of the male deer of different species, while others incorporate the scent gland fluids with extracts of apple, acorns, etc., all of which are intended to aid the hunter to stalk more successfully. (*See* "Hunting, Archery.")

Mail Match: An archery mail tournament or match is one which is conducted through the mails. Its purpose is to have widespread tournament competition which can be participated in by all archery club members belonging to or affiliated with an association which might sponsor such competition. The N.F.A.A. and the N.A.A. both sponsor this type of competitive shoots, and in both cases these tournaments are international events. The tournament may comprise a series of events shot over a period of several weeks, or it may include the aggregate scores of an entire year, but all shooting dates are required to be set and registered prior to the date of the events.

Trophies and awards are given by both of these associations and each association has a variety of events in which one may participate. (*See* "Rounds, Target Archery," "Rounds, Field Archery," and "Olympic Bowman League, O.B.L.")

Maclura Pomifera: The botanical name for Osage Orange, or Bois D'Arc. This wood is considered by modern bowyers as one of the finest bow woods available. Due to its extreme toughness and dense grain this wood will withstand far more abuse than any other bow wood. For this reason Maclura Pomifera (Osage Orange, Bois D'Arc) has been and still is the first choice for a fine hunting bow.

When first cut into, this wood is a brilliant yellow to an orange yellow color. With age the wood will gradually change color until it becomes a beautiful chestnut brown. Although bows made from this wood, even the most select, have a noticeable roughness or jar, one will soon become used to it, provided the bow is properly constructed to render a minimum of this fault.

Most bows made from Maclura Pomifera are usually thin, wider than is considered normal, and, in many cases, extremely short. The author has made many bows from 4 foot, 8 inches to 5 feet long which were capable of being drawn to 28" or 29". These were not always considered extreme cases either.

As the heartwood is the best of this species, the sapwood is and should be removed from the stave before any other work would be done on an osage bow.

This wood got its common names from the Osage Indians of Oklahoma and the French who called it Bois D'Arc (bwah dahark), which means bow wood.

Magazines, Archery: Following is a list of archery magazines available either by subscription or through club membership:

Archery Magazine: Published monthly. Official publication of the National Field Archers Association. $2.50 per year, U.S.A., $3.00 per year, foreign countries. P. O. Box H, Palm Springs, California.

The Archers Magazine T.A.M. Published monthly by The Archer's Publishing Company; official publication of the National Archery Association. $2.50 per year, U.S.A., $3.00 per year, foreign countries. 1200 Walnut Street, Philadelphia 7, Pennsylvania.

The Bowhunter. Published monthly. Official publication of the Wisconsin Bowhunters Association. Subscription through membership only. Magazine and dues per year $3.00. Send dues to Mrs. Evelyn Becker, 539 No. 99th Street, Milwaukee 13, Wisconsin.

The Broadhead. Published monthly. Official publication of the New York State Field Archery Association. Combined membership and subscription rate $3.00 per year. P. O. Box 311, Cooperstown, New York.

The Canadian Archer. Published monthly. The official publication of the Canadian Archery Association. $1.50 per year in Canada; U.S.A. and foreign countries, $1.75 per year. P. O. Box 1067, Vancouver 1, B.C.

The Eastern Bowhunter. Published monthly. $2.00 per year. The Eastern Bowhunter, Inc., Riverwood, Maryland.

The Michigan Bowman Magazine. Official publication of the

Michigan Bowhunters. $2.00 per year. Combination rate: magazine and membership is $3.00 per year. P. O. Box 127, Flint, Michigan.

The Nebraska Bowman. Official publication of The Prairie Bowman of Nebraska. Single copy rate is $.10. Membership in organization is $1.00 per year for individuals; $1.50 for families. 1858 Otoe Street, Lincoln 2, Nebraska.

The Northwest Archer. Published monthly. $1.75 per year. Sherman Spears, Editor, Box 2228, Portland, Oregon.

The Pacific Coast Bowhunter. Published monthly. $1.00 per year. P. O. Box 552, Encino, California.

Master Eye: The stronger of a person's two eyes or the one which registers the image on the brain. (*See* "Aiming Eye.")

Matched Shafts: In order that an archer may shoot his arrows and know that they will perform consistently through proper shooting techniques, one must shoot arrows which are matched. Arrows which are matched to one another in a complete set should all be very near to the same weight; i.e., within ten grains, or closer if possible, and the spine or stiffness should also be very nearly the same in relation to one another in the set. It makes no difference what kind of arrows the choice may be,—wood, glass or aluminum alloyed—the result will be the same with poorly matched arrows; a poor score. An archer who understands this will always choose the best grade of any kind of arrows that he selects.

A reasonably safe way to check the weight of a set of arrows is to use a "grain weight" chemical scale as most arrows produced today are weighed by the avoirdupois system.

To accurately check a set of arrows for spine or stiffness can only be done upon a spine tester which is graduated for proper bow weight and arrow spine relation; however, as a method of checking to find the relation of one arrow to another in a set, a two-pound weight with a padded hook attached to it may be hung upon the center of each shaft, which should be supported on each of its ends with blocks of wood. As each arrow is bent by the weight, the amount of the deflection can be measured. If the overall deflection variance is near to $\frac{1}{16}''$ or closer for all shafts, they will be quite well matched; however, if the variance goes upwards to $\frac{3}{16}''$ they may give considerable trouble, especially at the longer distances.

Matching Bins: A rack which is divided or one which has several separations for the specific purpose of assorting various groups of arrow shafts while they are in the process of being matched into sets. Different racks are usually used for grouping arrow shafts for spine than are used for the weight separation due to the different numbers used for each.

Matt: A round target butt or boss. Target matts are usually constructed from rye straw or marsh grass which has been tied into large rope-like strands and then coiled into a flat circular matt. Target matts must be very firm and tightly sewn together to elimi-

The championship medal (left) awarded to winners of the National championship tournaments is the "Dallin Medal." It is 3" in diameter and nearly ¼" thick. The championship medal of the N.F.A.A. was designed by the late William Burton Westcott, who donated the dies to the association for future use. The inscription, SAGGITTARIO DIGNISSIMO DATUR: "To the most worthy archer, this is given." The medal is gold in color, and is 1½" in diameter.

nate arrows from passing through them. These matts are available in many sizes for various kinds of archery rounds.

Medals, N.A.A.: Other than the Dallin medal shown here, there are the "Thompson Medal of Honor, The J. Maurice," "Six-Golds Pins," and "Range Buttons," all shown and explained under these headings.

Medals, N.F.A.A.: Other than the Championship medal shown here, there are "Art Young Big and Small Game Awards," "Compton Medal of Honor," "Compton Sportsman's Medal," and "Twenty Pin (National)," all of which are illustrated and explained under these headings. The N.F.A.A. Stump medal is shown under the heading "Associations (National)," Part (2) in the history of the N.F.A.A., 1941.

Membership, Honorary: A membership which may be bestowed upon a person, not necessarily a club member, but to anyone who has rendered an outstanding service to a club which is worthy of honorable recognition. This type of membership does not necessarily require a further service or duty by the person or persons holding same. An Honorary Membership is usually one which is dated for some period of time; not necessarily a life membership.

Membership, Life: A membership which shall be extended for the remainder of one's life. Memberships of this nature may be granted as an honor for outstanding service to a club, or an organization, or it may be one which is a paid membership.

Metropolitan Round: While this round is not one which is adopted for tournament shooting by the N.A.A., it is a very good round for keeping in practice from all of the longer distances and it requires less time to shoot than a York round. The distance which must be walked to shoot a York round is 4,160 yards while the Metropolitan round requires only 3,300 yards of walking. The round is as follows:

            5 ends—30 arrows—from 100 yards.
            5 ends—30 arrows—from 80 yards.
            5 ends—30 arrows—from 60 yards.
            5 ends—30 arrows—from 50 yards.
            5 ends—30 arrows—from 40 yards.

Momentum of an Arrow: That quality of its motion of flight which resists its being brought to rest after which it has been set into movement by the propelling force of the bow transmitted to the arrow through the medium of the bowstring.

N.A.A.: The National Archery Association of the United States of America. (*See* "Associations, National.")

N.F.A.A.: The National Field Archery Association of the United States of America. (*See* "Associations, National.")

National Round (for ladies): This is a very easy round as far as the distance required to walk and the number of arrows to be shot. A total of 960 yards is all that is required to walk and the number of arrows to be shot is 72. The round is as follows:

8 ends—48 arrows—from 60 yards.
4 ends—24 arrows—from 50 yards.

Naturally Reflexed: Bows which are naturally reflexed have limbs which return to a reverse bend after the bow is unstrung. This type of bow is made from the side or section of a log which was slightly bowed. The concaved side of the log would in this case be the back of the bow. A reflexed bow is usually somewhat faster in its acceleration or cast, but in many cases bows which are deeply reflexed are not smooth to shoot; i.e., they usually have a definite jar when they reach the end of the string after the release. (*See* "Reflexed Bow.")

Near, or Semi and Completely Center Shot Bows: Allow one tip end of a braced bow to rest on a finger tip while the other tip rests on the edge of a table. Sight the bowstring in a manner which puts it to the center of the bow limbs and the handle grip. Immediately above the bow handle one will notice that the string will appear to be *almost* along the side of a "near center shot bow" which accounts for this expression. If the bow is a completely center shot bow, the string will be *completely* to the side of the bow's upper limb where the arrow passes the bow. With either of these bow types a person is able to have a better view of his target while aiming. Another point to remember is that arrow spine is not as critically important as with a conventional bow where the string centers the bow limbs and its handle for the entire length of the bow. (*See* "Paradox, Archers.")

Neophyte: A beginner; one who is a novice. A novice archer is then a beginner or a neophyte.

N.A.A. Rounds: The following target rounds are shot in national tournament competition to decide the National Champions.
N.A.A. National Tournament Rounds.

(1) American Round for ladies, men and intermediates:
   American Round, Jr. for junior girls and junior boys.
   Clout round (180 yards) for men.
   Clout round (140 yards) for ladies.
   Clout round (120 yards) for ladies, intermediate and junior
      girls and boys.
   Columbia round for ladies.
   Columbia round, Jr. for beginner girls and boys.
   Hereford round: required round for intermediate boys and a
      choice round for ladies.
   International Long and Short rounds for men.
   International Long and Short rounds for ladies.
      Note: The ladies and men shoot the same Short Round.
   National Round for ladies and intermediate girls.
   Team Round (for ladies): ladies only.
   Team Round (for men): men.
   York Round for men.
   York Round, English, for men.

(2) N.A.A. Crossbow Division:
   American Round for ladies and men.
   Clout Round (180 yards) for ladies and men.
   Kings Round for the three high contestants only.

N.F.A.A. Rounds: The purpose of the following round is primarily to teach an archer the art of judging distances instinctively and accurately for the purpose of hunting later if he wishes to do so. Whether the archer uses a sight or not, the element of estimation is still basic since no shooting positions are to have the distances to the targets shown. There are no moving targets on an approved N.F.A.A. round; however, these may be included in a regular Novelty Round (*See* "Novelty Round"). Scoring: The value of the scoring ring shall be 5 points for the entire white or inside circle which includes the aiming center. Three points are allowed for the outer circle. All arrows which touch a scoring ring of the next higher value shall be counted as such. Skids or glance shots shall not be counted. Any arrow which bounces from a target or passes through a target (if witnessed) may be counted as 3 points. An arrow which passes through the target face, but not completely through the butt can be forced back and counted to the score of the ring it passes through. *The arrow may not be pulled from the target butt and pushed back point first!* Note: Four arrows are used.

N.F.A.A. Broadhead* Round: (scoring) The targets shall be scored as follows: If the first arrow hits the bull's-eye, it is 20; if it hits any other place within the scoring area, it is 15. Second arrow, bull's-eye 15, outside of bull's-eye in scoring area 10. Third arrow, bull's-eye 10, outside of bull's-eye in scoring area 5. After scoring with any arrow, you must not shoot again. Note: Only three arrows may be used; these may be, by direction, either field arrows or broadheads, or both.

N.F.A.A. Hunter's Round: (scoring) Score as is explained for the N.F.A.A. field round. The target face for this round is all black with very fine white lines which renders them undistinguishable from a short distance. Note: Four target arrows, or four field arrows, are used, depending upon the decision of the field captain.

Note: The various ranges which are used for these three rounds are outlined under "Archery Ranges," part (2).

Nocking Point of a Bowstring: The point on a bowstring which is at a right angle from the bowstring to the arrow rest. If the nocking point is located correctly, the nocked arrow, when setting on the arrow rest, and the bowstring will be at right angles to one another, or the arrow shaft will be perpendicular to the undrawn string.

The nocking point on a bowstring is a danger point to check on frequently. If at any time the string serving appears to have a spiraled raise on its surface, remove the string immediately as this

---

* The N.F.A.A. Broadhead round as of the national tournament of 1955 has been altered to thereafter be known as the Big Game Round due to the tremendous danger of a shoot of this type where so many participants take part.

N.F.A.A. Big Game Round: This round is virtually the same as the N.F.A.A. Broadhead round and until future notice from the N.F.A.A. officials will take the place of the Broadhead round. The same type of targets are used; however, since the N.F.A.A. National tournament of 1955 the official tournament committee has ruled out the use of broadheads due to the great danger involved with gatherings of that size. Regular field arrows matched to hunting arrows will be used until future notice in the Big Game Round. The type of targets will remain the same as those used previously for the Broadhead Round; i.e., animals, birds, or reptile type.

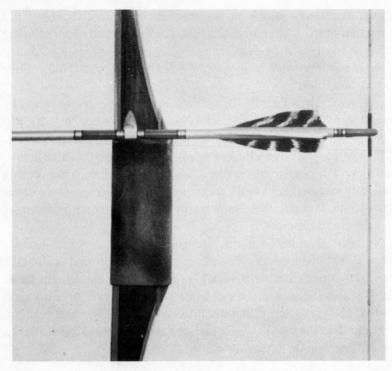

The nocking point on a bowstring. This fixed point eliminates the movement of the arrow up or down the string while the drawing takes place.

is the indication of a broken strand which in most cases has broken under the serving at the nocking point. (*See* Nomenclature and Drawing of the Bowstring.)

Nocking the Arrow: When one nocks an arrow, he places the nock of the arrow upon the bowstring at the nocking point; at that time the bow and arrow are ready for use. There are two methods of nocking an arrow and each has its place in archery.

(1) The conventional method, the method which is most commonly used is accomplished as follows: (A) grasp the bow in the bow hand with the bowstring above the bow and horizontal to the ground, (B) lay an arrow over the top side of the bow's upper limb on the arrow rest, holding the arrow by the nock with thumb and index finger of the string hand, (C) place the index finger of the bow hand lightly over the arrow shaft to hold it against the bow, (D) slide the arrow downwardly until the nock is laying on top of the bowstring nocking point. (E) At this point the index

Conventional method; Battle method.

finger which is under the arrow nock may be slipped under the bowstring while the thumb keeps the nock in position "D." (F) The thumb and index finger may then again hold the arrow nock while it is placed onto the nocking point of the string. The arrow will then be ready to draw, but—caution, before the draw is started, the index finger of the bow hand must be returned to the position on the bow handle where it belongs. Don't start the draw while holding the arrow against the side of the bow with the index finger of the bow hand or the arrow will be immediately de-nocked.

(2) Battle method: This method was very popular in ancient days when archers were in battle, usually because of the limited amount of space between the archers. This method is also used by hunting archers while in "close quarters" and is accomplished as follows: (A) Hold the bow vertically in shooting position, (B) bend the elbow and with the bowstring against the inside of the forearm lay the bow against the chest, (C) hold an arrow below the feathers about midway on the shaft and lay it over the arrow rest with the arrow nock towards the nocking point on the string; (D) slide the arrow over the rest until the nock is seated on the bow string at the nocking point. Note: When this method is used the arrow rest will be on the side of the bow which is away from the body. (E) The index finger of the bow hand may be used to hold the arrow onto the bow while the bow arm is again returned to shooting position, and *until* the draw is started.

Nock File: A nock file is a small round file usually referred to as a "rat tail" or "round bastard." This file in a $\frac{5}{32}''$x5" file is an ideal file to use to fashion the bow nocks on the tip ends of a bow.

Nock Locks: A recent idea which has merit. These are small live rubber tubes about ¼" long which are slipped onto a bowstring and placed on either side of a bowstring nocking point. If several of these are placed together, a shooting glove may be eliminated.

Nock Tapering Tool: A tool used to taper an arrow shaft to receive a replaceable plastic arrow nock. This operation may be done by sanding the shaft to a taper in a special jigg made specifically for this use, by cutting with a sharp knife, or by using a special tapering tool made for this use which closely resembles a hand operated pencil sharpener. Note: This is called a "nock tennon" or a "tapered nock tennon."

Nocks, Replaceable Arrow: (*See* "Arrow Nocks" or "Self Nocks.") Replaceable arrow nocks have come into great demand in the past twenty years, and are almost used exclusively now. These nocks are of many designs and are made by the injection mold process from many types of flexible plastics such as cellulose and acetates. There are many designs of these arrow nocks; however, they all feature the small raised rib which is called the "index" and which is placed directly behind the cock feather.

Nocks, Replaceable Bow: As is the case of the replaceable arrow nock, the replaceable bow nock is made from molded plastics; however, the replaceable bow nock no longer enjoys the same popularity. An applied bow nock of the replaceable design is almost out of style with exception of the use to which they are put on some glass bows. These nocks are easily broken from a bow and in many cases this will happen at a time when a person can least afford the inconvenience. (*See* "Self Nocks.")

Node: A node is a joint of two sections of bamboo, and appears as a small bump on the surface of the bamboo. A pole will have many nodes appearing on the surface. The spacing will depend entirely upon the species and its size.

The nodes of a bamboo bow backing should never be flattened off, but should only be slightly rounded to remove the soft pulpy layer where the leaf was joined to the node.

Non-Conventional Bow Riser: A riser of this type is one which either, partially or completely projects beyond the general straight line formed by the back of the bow. A bow of this type is seen in Fig. 15; another example of these bows is in "Bow Types." (*See* "Conventional Bow.")

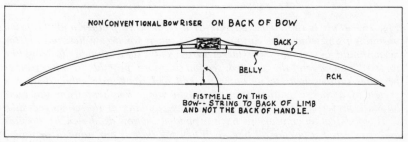

Fig. 15.—This type of bow design lends to stability of action. Such is the case in the Deflexed bow design where the handle does not tend to twist as the bow's limbs are being bent.

Novelty Round: Every club or group of archers has some time or another given their club shoots an added color by the substitution of one or more novelty events. These rounds may vary from a "ham shoot" to a "turkey or bacon shoot" and the targets may vary from shooting at a deck of cards pasted to a cardboard backstop to shooting through a round cardboard tube at a target face behind the tube. But basically a novelty round is to create a bit of added enjoyment to a tournament. These events are usually "dreamed up" by the club members and are accepted by the tournament committee. (*See* "N.F.A.A. Rounds.")

Novice: A neophyte or a beginner. One who requires instruction by an advanced archer. A novice's continued interest will depend upon the amount of guidance he receives from the advanced members of a group (and should never be taken lightly).

Oil Line (feather): A wing tip feather from a large bird such as a turkey, etc., will have a heavy padded mid-section on its vanes. This is noticeable only from the concaved side of a feather and is preferred due to the extra body and the natural oil which lends to the flexibility of the feather vane. The oil line appears to start near

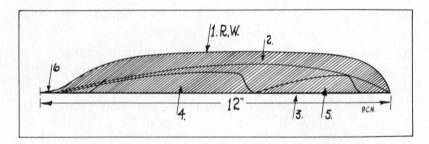

Fig. 16.—This is the concaved side of a right wing feather and the usual positions from which the various cuts are taken for arrow fletching. If the need should be for all short target arrow cuts, these should be from the forward end where the padded section is more prominent. The feather becomes thinner near to its outer tip end and is of little value. This is a sketch of a turkey feather from the right wing. Feathers from the male bird are preferred. 1. A right wing feather, looking at the concaved side. 2. A good feather appears to have a padded section as shown by the line and is referred to as the oil line. 3. When the base is cut, sanded or milled to a uniform thickness, it is referred to as a "base ground" feather. 4. A popular design for field or hunting arrows. The long length is necessary to control the weight of the heads used. 5. A smaller cut, more for use of target arrows but of the same design as that of number 4. 6. The front, or quill, end of the feather.

to the front or quill end of a feather and makes a parabolic curve for about three-fourths of the length of the feather and then returns again to the feather base where it again becomes very thin and flimsy. Arrow vanes should be cut from this portion of a feather as shown in Fig. 16.

Olympic Bowman League (O.B.L.): This league is sponsored by the N.A.A. and is the only indoor winter mail match competition of its kind recognized as official within the ranks of target archers in the United States. These matches are international events and are to determine the world champions for the Chicago and Olympic rounds with divisions for both sight and instinctive shooters. In 1957 this League celebrated its thirtieth anniversary.

The competition consists of the following two distinctly different rounds, the Olympic Round and the Chicago Round.

(1) The Olympic Round was the original of these two and was necessary because of the limited space available to archers in large cities. The Olympic Round (adult) consists of the following:

90 arrows (15 ends) from 30 yards at a 48″ target. This round must be shot by all members who have reached or passed their twelfth birthday. Members who have not reached their twelfth birthday are classed as follows:

Cadets: from eighth birthday until the twelfth birthday.

Cubs: All archers under eight years of age.

Cubs and Cadets shall shoot the Olympic Round as follows: 90 arrows (15 ends) from 20 yards at a 48″ target.

In the case of participating high school and college students, they shall shoot in the same classification group as the Adult round requires, or over the age of twelve years.

(2) The request of a group of Chicago archers was what brought the Chicago Round into being. The Chicago Round: In 1946 this round was adopted by the N.A.A. and was added to the indoor competition and is shot by adults as follows:

96 arrows (16 ends) from 20 yards at a 16″ target.

Cadets and Cubs shall shoot the Chicago Round as follows: 96 arrows (16 ends) from 15 yards at a 24″ target.

The Olympic Bowman League has divisions for all sizes and ages, and for all styles of shooting. Now they even have a special division for instinctive archers.

Other information regarding changes may be had by writing to
the N.A.A. Secretary or to the Olympic Bowman League, Mrs.
Florence Lilly, 5354 W. Oakdale Avenue, Chicago 41.

Olympic Round: (*See* "Olympic Bowman League, O.B.L.")

Optics for Archery: Courtesy of D. P. Bushnell and Company,
116 Bushnell Building, Pasadena 1, California.

One cannot be told, but must experience the pleasure of using
either a good Monocular, Binocular, or Spotting scope, in order
to find what a great convenience these optics are to archery.

For target archery any of the previously mentioned types of
optics is most helpful for checking arrow positions on targets at the
longer ranges. Considerable time and a great deal of unnecessary
walking can be saved while checking sights or points of aim.

For hunting or field shooting one is sure to find that a Binocular
or Monocular is as essential to "doing the job right" as the favorite
hunting bow or the precisely matched set of arrows. One must
remember that to hunt with proper optics is not to look at the tree
limbs, branches or bushes, but actually to look through them.
This is easier than it sounds as the stereoscopic effect of the instrument literally brushes the trees aside and one will see brightly-lit
pockets polka-dotted between the dark masses of trees, bushes and
shadows.

Relax your eyes and your temperament for this work. Get down
low and scan the surface of the ground under the branches. It is
easier to see between the tree trunks than through a thick mass of
tree branches. To look for unusual movement, inquisitive sniffing
noses; for ears, a tail or searching eyes, is to properly use an optic
for archery hunting. One's skill will increase with every hour of
intelligent practice. Note: It is suggested that the 7x35 power glass
be used for your archery. This optic will give excellent magnifi-
cation without being too critical to slight movement.

Osage Orange: (*See* "Maclura Pomifera.")

Over Bowed: An archer who is termed "over bowed" is one who
tries to shoot a bow which is of a drawing weight to some degree
more than can be efficiently and comfortably handled.

Over-draw: An over-draw is an extension to the rear portion of an
arrow rest. Its purpose is to allow an archer to draw a shorter

arrow than that which would be his normal full draw. An extreme example of this follows: An archer who normally shoots a 28" arrow may install an over-draw extension to his bow which would safely support the point end of a 24" arrow (this is a common practice with flight shooters). This archer may then draw with reasonable safety the shorter arrow of 24" length to his complete full draw of 28". The purpose is—to increase arrow spine by the shorter shaft and by the same token reduce the weight of the shaft as well as the resistance, which together add up to longer shots by the gain of greater speed.

Overlays: In the construction of some bows the overlays are used as a precautionary measure to tie down the facings and the backings at their ends. This is accomplished by filing completely through the plastic on a long taper of approximately 1½" to the inner wood lamination but not to exceed a depth of $\frac{1}{32}$" below the under side of the facing or backing. This will allow gluing the overlay, wood or plastic, partially to the wood lamination rather than completely to the glass or plastic facing. Some overlays are merely for appearance rather than as tie-downs.

Paradox, Archers: As the arrow spine is directly related to "The Archers Paradox," it should be clearly understood by all who shoot the bow and arrow. Paradoxical means a thing or a statement which, even though it is seemingly absurd or self-contradictory, actually can happen. This is the case of the arrow passing the side of the bow. If the spine is correct for the bow, it will cause the arrow to be in direct alignment with the exact center of the bow limbs a short distance from the back of the bow, as though it were shot directly through the center of the bow's limb rather than around the side of the limb or handle. Note: The more nearly a bow string aligns to the side of the bow which the arrow passes, as in the case of the "near center," or "complete center shot" bow, the less the "Archers Paradox" will affect one's shooting; however, even with a complete center shot bow one's arrows must be of proper spine or stiffness to withstand the thrust of the bow.

Parallel Pile: A target point made of metal or molded plastic with a hole which is bored parallel to its sides and its sides parallel to each other. The points have a sharp conical type pointed end. (*See* "Arrow Pile," and "Arrow Points.")

Passing Arrow: (N.A.A. Target Scoring) An arrow which has completely passed through a target butt or matt shot from either 80 or 100 yards shall be counted as a blue, or 5 points; arrows which pass through a target from 60 yards or less shall count as a red, or 7 points. All passing arrows must be witnessed by a target mate or a field official to be counted. (*See also* "N.F.A.A. Field Round: scoring.")

Peep Sight: A bow sight which has a small peep hole through at least one of the two ends of the horizontal aiming bar. The other end may be a pin type or another peep hole.

Perfect End: To shoot six arrows consecutively into the gold or bull's-eye in any one end is to shoot a score of 54 or a "Perfect End." If a person is a member of the N.A.A., and if the tournament is a regular six-golds one, of either the long bow (regular target archers) or the crossbow division, the archer's score card may be signed and properly filled out for official recognition by the N.A.A. By proper recognition, it should be understood that a beautiful six-golds pin will be awarded six-golds shooters when the circumstances are as they should be.

Pistol Grip Handle: This new design of a bow handle is specifically made for archers who use the "tilted hand" or "locked wrist" method of holding their bow, (*See* "Bow Hand Grip," part (3)) and comprises a short handle projecting slightly downward on the inside of the bow, and is an addition to and a new conception of the regular saddle handle. Its purpose is to allow an archer to close his fingers under the short grip rather than along the sides of the regular type handle. (See modification of this grip in "Handle Types.")

Pin Knot: A small tight knot in a bow stave. These small defects do not necessarily mean that a stave is unworthy of a bow. Yew wood and Osage Orange are examples of this statement as both woods make excellent bows and in many cases either may have several small tight pins. It should not be forgotten that these small pins should *not* appear on or near to the edge of a bow's limb as the wood between the pin and the bow's edge may fracture, thus causing the bow to splinter from this point.

Pin Stripes: To separate the distinctive colors of an arrow crest, fine decorative pin stripes or lines are painted on the shaft. Arrow crests which are trimmed with these small dainty lines are far more attractive than arrows without pin stripes for trim.

Plastic Arrow Nocks: (*See* "Nocks, Replaceable Arrow.")

Plastic Bow Nocks: Bow nocks which are made from molded plastic but not necessarily an integral part of the bow's tip ends. (*See* "Nocks, Replaceable.")

The string hand should never leave the face unless the archer draws to the side of the face, in which case the hand may move backwards upon the release of the string tension.

Plastic Fletching: This type of arrow vane is not altogether new, but is gaining in popularity due to the seasonal shortages of good feathers, also the fact that plastic vanes will withstand a great deal of abuse and remain in excellent condition. Plastic fletching is very popular in damp weather and for use on fishing arrows, since it is waterproof and needs no special water repellant. These vanes are made of a very thin pliable molded plastic which appears to have very small corrugations to induce rigidity. (*See* "Feathers (arrow)" and "Vanes.")

Plucking the String: This fault or habit is one which will give an archer considerable trouble as it is actually part of the loose or release. When one plucks the bowstring he releases it in a jerky motion which sets it into side vibrations. This in turn will cause the arrow to flutter or fishtail in a zigzag motion and will vary as the plucking of the string is never consistently the same. One should simply allow the fingers to relax and allow the string to slide off of the finger tips smoothly and never jerk the string hand away from the face sideways.

Point Blank: At point blank range, immediately before the release, the full drawn arrow point will appear to be exactly on the bull's-eye when the archer aims his arrow. Every bow and set of arrows will have a point blank range from some distance or another. Every archer should know the exact distance from which he will be able to shoot his bow at point blank range. Any and all distances less than point blank range will allow the target to be visible and above the bow hand. From all distances beyond point blank range one will note that the hand, the lower bow limb, or the bow arm will, to some degree, cover the target. The speed, cast, or acceleration of a bow, the weight of the arrows in use, and the distance that an archer anchors his arrow below the aiming eye all govern the distance from which a bow is termed "Point Blank." (*See* "Instinctive or Space Aiming.")

Point of Aim: Note: While the range finder is not a part of this method of shooting, it is essential that it not be separated from the explanation of this type of shooting to avoid further confusion. Therefore, please note that "Point of Aim Range Finder" follows this explanation.

For regular target archery it is advisable to use the low anchor

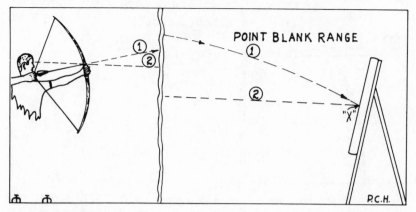

Fig. 17.—*Point blank range: This varies with the speed, cast, or accelera-*
tion of a bow. A bow which is of a light drawing weight that has fast
acceleration may have the same point blank range as a heavier drawing bow
which is of less cast. When shooting from point blank range, raise your
bow hand until you are looking directly over your arrow point at the spot
you wish to hit. 1. Dotted line number 1 is the path of the arrow. 2. Dotted
line number 2 is the vision line of the eye. 3. The point marked "X" is the
point blank point of aim.

point, under the point of or to the side of the chin as the point of
aim will be visible or below the bull's-eye for a greater distance
than it would for a high draw or corner of the mouth anchor, such
as is used for space or instinctive aiming.

(1) To first range in a bow for a point of aim a person should
stand straddle of a line which is perpendicular to the line of an
arrow's flight to the target. (2) Place a peg at the toe of each shoe
to locate the exact position of each foot. (3) Now measure the
exact distance that you draw your arrow nock below your eye to
the anchor point at the side or point of your chin; this space is
the distance which the bull's-eye should appear above the full
drawn arrow point while shooting from approximately 10 yards.
(Note: This space must be decreased approximately ½ inch to $\frac{9}{16}$
inch for each ten yards increased distance. The cast of a bow, the
weight of the arrows in use, and the location of the anchor point
will govern the measurement of these spacings.) (4) After checking on steps 1, 2, and 3, the arrow must be carefully drawn to full
draw and properly anchored against the face. (5) Rather than
release the arrow, the shooter should then look directly over the
arrow point to the ground. At this spot on the ground the point

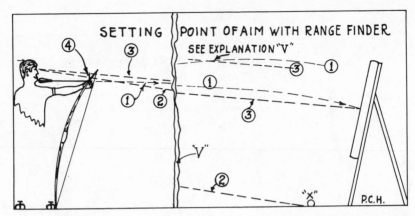

Fig. 18.—Setting the point of aim with a range finder. 1. The path of the
arrow to the target after it has been shot. 2. Vision line from eye looking
alongside of one of the ranger finder markings. 3. Line of eye's vision
looking over the top, or past the marking labeled *GOLD* to the bull's-eye.
4. The range finder stick steadied upon upper bow limb. ("V") This is the
space which is omitted from the drawing. The explanation is to show that
the arrow will always cross the lines 2 or 3; i.e., in setting your point of
aim look over the arrow point to the point of aim, on line 6. The arrow
crosses line 3 in flight to get to the target.

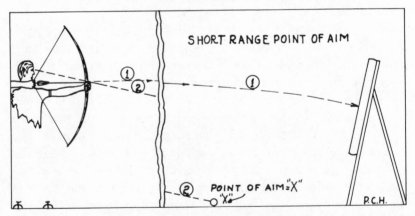

Fig. 19.—Short range point of aim: The nearer the archer is to his target,
the closer his point of aim will be to him; thus the lower the bow hand
must be; i.e., when the archer reaches a distance which will allow him to
look directly alongside of his bow at the bull's-eye and see a space between
his arrow point and the bull's-eye equal to the exact distance he has drawn
his arrow below his eye, no greater correction can be made without shooting too low. This distance (usually ten yards) will vary directly with the
cast of the bow and the weight of the arrows. 1. Dotted line 1 is the path
of the arrow. 2. Dotted line 2 is the vision line of the eye. 3. The point
marked "X" is the point of aim on the ground and between the archer and
the target.

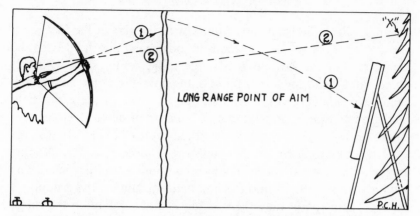

Fig. 20.—Long range point of aim: Find this point vertically above your bull's-eye in a tree top, on a roof, etc. A few practice shots carefully planned will usually be all which are necessary to find a correct point of aim at long range. 1. Dotted line 1 is the path of the arrow. 2. Dotted line 2 is the vision line of the eye. 3. The point marked "X" in the trees is the long range point of aim. Note: For windage correction a point may have to be found to the right or left of the bull's-eye.

of aim should then be placed. A small ball or round disc easily visible from the shooting position may be used. (6) When the point of aim is in place, return to the toe markers, draw to full draw, look directly over the arrow point at the point of aim, and release the string smoothly but crisply. (7) If the arrow falls short when released, move the point of aim a few feet nearer to the target; vice versa if the arrow goes high. (8) If the arrow goes to the left side on the target, move back from the toemarkers a few inches; if the arrow goes to the right on the target, move your toe markers a few inches ahead. (9) After the point of aim is located correctly, it should be used for all shots which follow from this distance. (10) Before moving to another shooting position of greater distance, the location of the point of aim should be recorded to a point of aim range finder stick. (*See* "Aiming a Bow and Arrow" and explanations and drawings of the point of aim which follow and the preceding explanations of "Point Blank.")

Point of Aim Range Finder: How to make and use the range finder for point of aim shooting.

A range finder stick is made as follows: Make a small stick ⅛" to ¼" thick, by ¾" wide and 6 inches to 6½ inches long. Make a very small hole ½" from one end, just large enough to push the point of the arrow into. After placing the arrow point in the hole, one may place the lower tip of his bow to the side of the foot nearest the target (Fig. 18). Extend the bow hand and hold both the upper end of the bow limb and the range finder stick with this same hand. With the arrow point in the hole, the range finder stick held perpendicular to the ground, and the nock of the arrow held to the anchor point, move the bow hand up or down the bow limb until the top end of the stick marked GOLD (Fig. 21) will be exactly in the center of the bull's-eye (dotted line 3). As one might look along the side of the range finder (dotted line 2) he would then see the location of the point of aim on the ground. A record of this point may then be marked accurately on the range finder (point 4 Fig. 18). After referring to the note following step 3 of the "Point of Aim" method of shooting a bow and arrow, move back to 30 yards and repeat this procedure. Mark the range finder for 30 yards, and recheck by trial and error until the point of aim is exactly located. Divide this space between 10 and 30 yards and this new mark will be for 20 yards. The distance be-

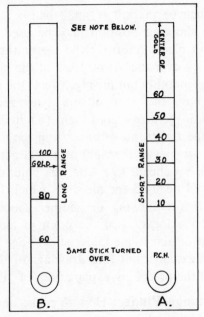

Fig. 21.—This example of a range finder is for a 52-pound bow. All marks indicated are for one particular bow and set of arrows matched thereto. Each bow should have a separate range finder for every different set of arrows to be used with that particular bow, or that the markings should be in different colors for alternate sets; i.e., set number one, green marks; set number two, black marks, etc.

tween 10 and 20, or 20 and 30 yards on the range finder will be the same for each 10 yards thereafter to at least 60 yards. (*See* Figs. 17, 18 and 19.)

To record points of aim which would be above or beyond the target, this same range finder may be turned over. Follow this by drawing a mark across the lower end of the stick about 3″ above the arrow point hole and label this mark "GOLD." Proceed as before but find the various points of aim either above the bull's-eye on the upper part of the target face or in a tree behind the target. Record these points for 60, 80 and 100 yards by holding the line marked GOLD on the center of the bull's-eye. Mark the range finder as before. (See drawing of range finder for a 52# bow. *See* Fig. 21, "B.")

Point Tapering Tool: This tool is used to taper the front of an arrow shaft to properly receive the arrow points which have tapered holes. This tool is similar to a hand operated pencil sharpener as is the nock tapering tool. Shafts may also be tapered for this type of point on a special sand tapering jigg. This process is called making a tapered point tennon.

Point Tennon Tool, for Parallel Points: This tool has either a cutter similar to an end mill, or an adjustable blade which is used to reduce the size of the forward end of an arrow shaft to receive an arrow point which has a hole parallel to its sides. A point tennon of this type weakens an arrow to a degree. With a glancing hit on a target stand, many an arrow point has been broken from the shaft. Points which have been spun on, or where the shaft is actually compressed to a smaller size to receive the point, are much less likely to break from shock.

Points, Insert Type: *See* in "Arrow Points," part (1), (b).

Pop-up Targets: Many archery clubs will have novelty events along with their tournament shooting. These events include various movable targets, one of which is a pop-up target. This type of target is to simulate life-like movements of various types of game and is a means of acquiring rapid coordination for hunting.

Pouch: A small auxiliary pocket attached to the belt or quiver. Its use is to carry lunches or small accessories in rather than in the pockets.

Practice Ends: (A) Prior to a regular scheduled target archery tournament a period of time is held open for archers to shoot a few practice ends which are uninterrupted. These ends are usually limited to three in number preceding a round, and from the longest distance which will be shot in that round. Other incidents which have a bearing on practice ends are rainfall, storms, lunch periods, accidents, or in some cases when a tournament has to be continued on a following day because of darkness. The situation and the total time which is interrupted have a direct relation as to the number of special practice ends allowed. Practice ends in target archery are shot upon the target to which the archers are assigned. (B) In field archery there are special areas set aside for practice only and in no case is an archer allowed to practice on a tournament range prior to the starting time for that tournament.

"Prima Donna": This term is one which is used occasionally in archery to signify one who has an air of untouched ability but not necessarily of the feminine sex. The term is also sometimes used to signify the erratic path of a specific arrow while in flight, or an arrow which, although seemingly like all others in a set, cannot be shot with like results for some reason or another.

Prism Lens: Bow sights which have a prism lens are those whose aiming lenses are ground to varied degrees of bevels to be used on bows of varied casts. A prism lens allows an archer to aim a bow of the lighter drawing weights and still have the aiming bar safely above the arrow rest. The lens usually has a very fine crosshair line or a small dot etched or painted on the center of the lens. The adjustment for a prism sight is the same as for a plain glass lens. These sights are used by target archers who prefer the sight to the point of aim method of shooting. (*See* "Bow Sight.")

Archers who use a prism type sight must be very careful while aiming from the longer distances that they do not shoot onto the wrong target which does happen at times. (*See* "Bow Sight.")

Prod: A word used erroneously to name a crossbow arrow, bolt or quarrel.

Professional Archer: One who makes archery his vocation; or an archer who at any time has received money as an award for his score in any kind of archery event, other than as a door or drawing prize.

Quarrel: An arrow for use in a crossbow, a crossbow bolt.

Quartered Logs: Logs which have been split or sawed into quarters to speed up the seasoning period. All log sections should be sealed on the surface to eliminate rapid drying which in turn causes checks and splits.

Quartering: Has reference to a breeze or wind which may blow at right angles to the shooting lanes of an archery range, or at a quartering angle to the path of an arrow while in flight.

Quill: The main stem of a feather. The hollow tube to which the feather vanes are attached. In the case of a prepared base ground or cut feather, the quill has been greatly reduced in size to a thin flat base which is perpendicular to the feather vanes.

Quiver: An arrow quiver is a device used specifically for carrying or holding arrows which may not be in immediate actual use. There are several kinds and each has its own qualities. (1) The Hip Pocket quiver is a heavy leather pocket liner used by either target or field archers when a minimum of arrows are to be carried. This type of a quiver eliminates damage to the trouser pockets and is very handy. (2) The ground quiver is one which is fashioned in many ways from steel rod in a manner which will not only hold a flight of arrows but will also act as a bow holder while the bow is not in use. The ground quiver has a sharp pointed end on the bottom of the main vertical rod which is forced into the turf a few inches. The upper end usually has a small circular loop and a pair of extended bent rods which serve as the arrow and bow supports respectively. (3) The back quiver is used by roving and field archers and is fashioned to be carried on the back. This type of quiver has a great many variations and sizes and is usually made to hold from one to three dozen field and hunting arrows. (4) A side quiver is sometimes similar and has the same basic function as the back quiver; however, this quiver is hung from the archer's belt which circles his waist. There are other types of side and back quivers designed to hold hunting arrows separated from one another in order that the sharp blades do not come into contact with each other. (5) The bow quiver is a quiver designed to fasten to the bow. This quiver is also fashioned to hold the arrows separated from each other but because of its very compact size is limited to carrying but a very few arrows, usually two or three. (See photos of quiver types.)

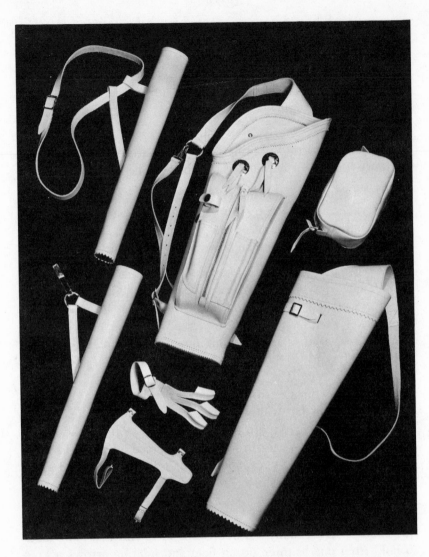

Some of the several types of quivers available today are these white accessories for ladies; target and field archery quivers, glove, armguard and pouch. (Photo courtesy of King-Sport Line Co.)

The back quiver (left) being put to practical use; A ground quiver as it is used for target archery. Note the bow rests on the side of the quiver next to the archer.

A new design for a side hunting quiver, designed by the author.

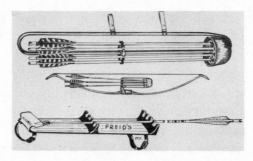

Fig. 22.—Three types of hunting quivers. Top is a Knipp Hip Quiver (courtesy of Chet Knipp); center is a Bear Bow quiver (courtesy of Bear Archery Co.); bottom is a Freid Arm quiver (by Robert A. Freid).

Range Buttons: These small pins are available from the N.A.A. to signify the distance from which an N.A.A. member may have won his Six-Golds pin. The pin is $\frac{7}{16}$ of an inch in diameter with gold lettering and trim, with colored background. The pins are available to beginners for 20 and 30 yards and to the senior divisions for 30, 40, 50 and 60 yards. The charge for these pins is $1.25 each and is assumed by the individual winner.

Range Finder for Point of Aim Shooting: A small slat of wood which is used for the purpose of recording points of aim for future use by archers who shoot the point of aim method. (*See* "Point of aim Rangefinder.")

Ranges for Field Archery: For Field, Broadhead and Hunter's ranges, refer to "Archery Ranges," part (2).

Ranges for Target Archery: Refer to "Archery Ranges," part (1).

"Razor Sharp Hunting Heads" (regardless of design): A hunting archer's "must" when broadheads are used. There have been many opinions expressed relative to the preference of razor sharp rather than "fair" sharpened hunting heads for years, many being very feasible reasons. Regarding the "razor sharp" broadhead preference, a few of these reasons are: (1) greater flesh and bone penetration, (2) greater possibility of severing small veins and arteries on contact, (3) better possibilities of internal and external hemorrhaging which lends to a more defined blood trail for tracking of wounded game, (4) less tissue injury from shock, (5) less chance of survival from seemingly non-critical hits. All of these issues are worth serious thought and consideration from a hunter's point of view. Some of the important drawbacks of poorly sharpened hunting heads are: (1) poor penetration of flesh or bone, (2) less ability to cut small veins and arteries on contact, (3) very poor chance of hemorrhage, unless in a strictly vital area such as cutting the jugular veins, (4) greater damage to the skin tissue which would induce more rapid blood coagulation, (5) dull blades passing through the stomach area may possibly tend to push intestines aside rather than to damage them seriously.

The question arises as to how to keep sharp hunting heads sharp. (1) Never practice with a blade you plan to hunt with unless you take particular pains to re-sharpen this blade. (2) A hunting quiver which will keep your blades separated from each other is very practical, and there are several types to choose from. (*See* "Quiver," "*Thrombin," "*Anti-coagulant," and "Serrated Blade.")

Rebounds: (1) In target archery, any arrow which rebounds from any part of the scoring area shall be counted as a red, or 7 points, except at the distances of 80 or 100 yards where it shall be counted as the score of the blue, or 5 points. All rebounds must be witnessed by at least one target mate or a tournament official to be valid.

(2) In field archery any arrow which rebounds from a target may be counted as 3 points, if witnessed.

Record Scores: In all national and/or club tournaments in affiliation with either of the national associations, it is the duty of the scoring committee to make the immediate record of any score which either ties or breaks any existing record. These statistics must be sent to either the National Archery Association or the National Field Archery Association, whichever the case may be, for recognition and recording.

Records, (standing): Field archery rounds as of the 1957 National N.F.A.A. Tournament.

STANDING NATIONAL TOURNAMENT RECORDS (1957)

Records of National Field Champions Shot Instinctively
(Bare Bow)

GIRLS: (All ages to 15 years, inclusive)

FIELD ROUND: *Year Score*
Carol Hastic, Passaic, N. J...1957   534

HUNTERS ROUND:
Carol Hastic 1957   517

BIG GAME ROUND:
Rhea Bauer, Belleville,
Mich. 1956   625

BROADHEAD ROUND:
Rhea Bauer 1955   660

AGGREGATE SCORE:
Carol Hastic 1957 1641

LADIES:

FIELD ROUND: *Year Score*
Frances Lozon, Marine
City, Mich. 1957   651

HUNTERS ROUND:
Jo McCubbins, Santa Ana,
Calif. 1956   704

BIG GAME ROUND:
Joan Fahlgren, Midland,
Mich. 1956   820

BROADHEAD ROUND:
Frances Lozon 1950   725

AGGREGATE SCORE:
Jo McCubbins 1956 2139

JUNIOR BOYS: (12 years and under)

FIELD ROUND: *Year Score*
J. Steven Beinhauer, Pittsburgh 1955   473

HUNTERS ROUND:
John Gatski, Grant Town,
W. Va. 1955   616

BIG GAME ROUND:
Jim Stewart, Muskegon,
Mich. 1957   585

BROADHEAD ROUND:
John Gatski 1955   890

AGGREGATE SCORE:
John Gatski 1955 1962

INTERMEDIATE BOYS:
(13, 14 and 15 years)

FIELD ROUND: *Year Score*
Thomas Lee Rice, San
Francisco 1957   742

HUNTERS ROUND:
Thomas Lee Rice 1957   781

BIG GAME ROUND:
Thomas Lee Rice 1957   870

BROADHEAD ROUND:
Gary Anderson, Charleroi,
Pa. 1954   930

AGGREGATE SCORE:
Thomas Lee Rice 1957 2393

MEN:

FIELD ROUND: *Year Score*
Jay Peake, Charleroi, Pa.....1957   886

HUNTERS ROUND:
Jay Peake 1957   886

BIG GAME ROUND:
Jay Peake 1957   975

BROADHEAD ROUND:
Erwin Ketzler, Flint, Mich...1951   915

AGGREGATE SCORE:
Jay Peake 1957 2747

FREE STYLE DIVISION RECORDS
(*Shot with Sights*)

GIRLS: (All ages to 15 years, inclusive)

FIELD ROUND: *Year* *Score*
Ann Marston, Wyandotte, Mich. 1953 618
HUNTERS ROUND:
Ann Marston 1953 644
BIG GAME ROUND:
Janet Leder, Cincinnati........1957 415
BROADHEAD ROUND:
Ann Marston 1953 690
AGGREGATE SCORE:
Ann Marston 1953 1952

BOYS: (All ages to 15 years, inclusive)

FIELD ROUND: *Year* *Score*
William Hicks, Glendale, Calif. 1952 749
HUNTERS ROUND:
William Hicks 1951 775
BIG GAME ROUND:
Kenny Smathers, Brevard, N. C. 1957 820
BROADHEAD ROUND:
William Hicks 1951 920
AGGREGATE SCORE:
William Hicks 1951 2379

LADIES:

FIELD ROUND: *Year* *Score*
Anyta E. Davies, Hermosa Beach, Calif. 1957 771
HUNTERS ROUND:
Ann Marston 1957 812
BIG GAME ROUND:
Cleo Roberson, Samaria, Mich. 1957 835
BROADHEAD ROUND:
Betty Lifford, Lansing, Mich. 1953 795
AGGREGATE SCORE:
Ann Marston 1957 2390

MEN:

FIELD ROUND:
Reuben Powell, Chula Vista, Calif. 1955 930
HUNTERS ROUND:
Reuben Powell 1955 941
BIG GAME ROUND:
Reuben Powell 1956 985
BROADHEAD ROUND:
Reuben Powell 1953 980
AGGREGATE SCORE:
Reuben Powell 1955 2796

HUNTER'S DIVISION RECORDS
Shot Instinctively (*Bare Bow*) with Heavy Tackle*

LADIES:

FIELD ROUND:
Esther Thompson, New Castle, Pa. 1957 322
HUNTERS ROUND:
Esther Thompson 1957 358
BIG GAME ROUND:
Faye A. Vanderhoef, Boise, Ida. 1956 555
AGGREGATE SCORE:
Esther Thompson 1957 1200

MEN:

FIELD ROUND:
Lowell Roper, Oakland, Calif. 1956 730
HUNTERS ROUND:
James Palmer, Dansville, N. Y. 1957 721
BIG GAME ROUND:
Tim Meigs, Oakland, Calif...1956 925
AGGREGATE SCORE:
Lowell Roper 1956 2303

* This division was instituted in 1956, which accounts for the fact that there are no records for the Broadhead round which was discontinued in 1955.

TARGET ARCHERY STANDING RECORDS

Records, (standing): Target archery as of the 73rd Annual 1957
National N.A.A. Tournament.

LADIES		Hits Score	Name	Year
Double National		144 — 1138	Jean Lee,	1950
Single National		72 — 578	Carole Meinhart,	1957
60 yards		48 — 382	Carole Meinhart,	1957
50 yards		24 — 202	Jean Lee,	1950
Double Columbia		144 — 1214	Carole Meinhart,	1957
Single Columbia		72 — 616	Ann Weber Corby,	1952
50 yards	tie {	24 — 202	Ann Weber Corby,	1955
		24 — 202	Carole Meinhart,	1956
40 yards		24 — 210	Jean Lee, Ann Weber Corby,	1952
30 yards		24 — 216	Ann Weber Corby,	1952
Double American		180 — 1476	Jean Lee,	1950
Single American		90 — 740	Jean Lee,	1950
60 yards		30 — 238	Jean Lee,	1950
50 yards		30 — 256	Jean Lee,	1951
40 yards	tie {	30 — 260	Jean Lee,	1950
		30 — 260	Artie Palkowski,	1957
Clout (140 yds.)	tie {	36 — 284	Virginia Hersh,	1955
		34 — 284	Eleanor Moczadlo,	1956
Clout (120 yds.)		36 — 310	Jean Lee,	1951
Hereford Round		143 — 1017	Ann Weber Corby,	1951
International Short Round		90 — 682	Ann Weber Corby,	1955
Team Round (96 arrows at 50 yds.)				
High Individual Score		96 — 764	Betty Gregg,	1953
Team Round (4 women)		380 — 2688	N. Detroit Archers,	1953

Flight:	Yds. Feet Ins.		
35 lb.	433 — 2 — 2	Mrs. Jack Stewart,	1948
50 lb.	505 — 0 — 0	Evelyn Haines,	1950
Unlimited	473 — 1 — 7	Verne Tritin,	1948
Free Style	575 — 2 — 0	Eunice Modlin,	1949

MEN:	Hits Score	Name	Year
Double York	285 — 1855	Sylvester Chessman,	1957
Single York	140 — 974	Joe Fries,	1955
100 yards	68 — 442	Joe Fries,	1955
80 yards	48 — 356	Russ Reynolds,	1949
60 yards	24 — 196	Pat Chambers,	1938
Double American	179 — 1505	Harold Doan,	1956
Single American	90 — 762	Joe Fries,	1956
60 yards	30 — 250	Harold Doan,	1956
50 yards	30 — 260	Joe Fries,	1957
40 yards	30 — 266	O. K. Smathers,	1953
Sextuple American Round	539 — 4229	Norman W. Richards,	1957
Single American	90 — 720	Norman W. Richards,	1957
English York	135 — 829	Carl Strang,	1941

International Long Round	143 — 911	Russ Reynolds, 1950
International Short Round	90 — 763	Joe Fries, 1955
Clout (180 yds.)	36 — 302	Robert Rhode, 1956
Team Round (96 arrows at 60 yds.)		
High Individual Score	96 — 794	Joe Fries, 1956
Team Round (4 men)	383 — 2885	Sacramento Archery Club, 1957

Flight:	Yds. Feet Ins.	
50 lb.	552 — 2 — 4	Jack Stewart, 1948
65 lb.	603 — 2 — 0	L. C. Haugan, 1949
80 lb.	640 — 0 — 0	Jack Stewart, 1949
Unlimited	625 — 1 — 8	Jack Stewart, 1948
Free Style	774 — 0 — 0	Charles Pierson, 1955

INTERMEDIATE BOYS 15—18:

	Hits Score	
Double Hereford Round	284 — 2042	Richard Carlson, 1955
Single Hereford	144 — 1064	Jim Yoakum, 1957
80 yards	72 — 478	Jim Yoakum, 1957
60 yards	48 — 392	Richard Carlson, 1954
50 yards	24 — 202	Jim Yoakum, 1957
Double American	180 — 1472	Jim Yoakum, 1957
Single American	90 — 738	Jim Yoakum, 1957
60 yards	30 — 244	David Peterson, 1956
50 yards	30 — 256	Richard Carlson, 1955
40 yards	30 — 262	Jim Yoakum, 1957
Clout (120 yds.)	36 — 300	Bert Corley, 1951

Flight:	Yds. Feet Ins.	
35 lb.	473 — 0 — 6	Larry Modlin, 1955
50 lb.	553 — 0 — 0	Larry Modlin, 1955
Unlimited	504 — 0 — 0	Larry Modlin, 1955

JUNIOR BOYS 12—15:

	Hits Score	
Quadruple Jr. American	360 — 2974	Robert Oxnam, Jr., 1957
Single Jr. American	90 — 752	Robert Oxnam, Jr., 1957
50 yards tie {	30 — 236	Kenny Smathers, 1956
	30 — 236	Robert Oxnam, Jr., 1957
40 yards	30 — 254	Robert Oxnam, Jr., 1957
30 yards tie {	30 — 266	Kenny Smathers, 1956
	30 — 266	Robert Oxnam, Jr., 1957
Clout (120 yds.)	36 — 256	Gerald Kapela, 1955

Flight:	Yds. Feet Ins.	
35 lb.	339 — 1 — 0	Jim Dillon, 1955
50 lb.	405 — 2 — 0	Jim Dillon, 1956
Unlimited	359 — 2 — 0	Jim Dillon, 1956

BEGINNER BOYS (Under 12 years):

	Hits Score	
Quadruple Jr. Columbia	288 — 2342	Joey Moeller, 1954
Single Jr. Columbia	72 — 594	Joey Moeller, 1954

	Hits	Score	Name	Year
40 yards	24 — 186		Joey Moeller,	1954
30 yards	24 — 198		Joey Moeller,	1954
20 yards	24 — 214		Alan Stafford,	1957

INTERMEDIATE GIRLS 15—18:

	Hits	Score	Name	Year
Double National	143 — 1071		Nancy Breneman,	1955
Single National	72 — 536		Nancy Breneman,	1955
60 yards	48 — 346		Nancy Breneman,	1955
50 yards	24 — 192		Nancy Breneman,	1955
Double Columbia	144 — 1144		Nancy Breneman,	1955
Single Columbia	72 — 580		Grace Frye,	1950
50 yards	24 — 184		Grace Frye,	1950
40 yards	24 — 208		Nancy Breneman,	1955
30 yards	24 — 210		Kay Volkman,	1957
Double American	179 — 1351		Kay Volkman,	1957
Single American	90 — 702		Kay Volkman,	1957
60 yards	30 — 222		Grace Frye,	1950
50 yards	30 — 238		Kay Volkman,	1957
40 yards	30 — 256		Kay Volkman,	1957
Clout (120 yds.)	36 — 298		Lorna Price,	1952

Flight:	Yds. Feet Ins.			
35 lb.	418 — 1 — 1		Peggy Dunway,	1946
50 lb.	427 — 2 — 9½		Peggy Dunway,	1946
Unlimited	393 — 1 — 10		Peggy Dunway,	1946

JUNIOR GIRLS 12—15:

	Hits	Score	Name	Year
Double Columbia	141 — 1109		Kay Volkman,	1956
Single Columbia	70 — 564		Kay Volkman,	1956
50 yards	23 — 175		Kay Volkman,	1956
40 yards	24 — 184		Janet Leder,	1956
30 yards	24 — 206		Kay Volkman,	1956
Double Jr. American	180 — 1456		Kay Volkman,	1956
Single Jr. American	90 — 736		Kay Volkman,	1956
50 yards	30 — 236		Kay Volkman,	1956
40 yards	30 — 248		Kay Volkman,	1956
30 yards	30 — 260		Kay Volkman,	1956
Clout (120 yds.)	36 — 272		Janet Leder,	1956

Flight:	Yds. Feet Ins.			
35 lb.	267 — 0 — 0		Bertha Modlin,	1955

BEGINNER GIRLS (Under 12 years):

	Hits	Score	Name	Year
Quadruple Jr. Columbia	288 — 2402		Loy E. Volkman,	1957
Single Jr. Columbia	72 — 606		Loy E. Volkman,	1957
40 yards	24 — 196		Loy E. Volkman,	1957
30 yards	24 — 208		Loy E. Volkman,	1957
20 yards	24 — 214		Loy E. Volkman,	1957

CROSSBOW STANDING RECORDS

Records, (standing): Crossbowmen as of the 1957 National N.A.A. Tournament.

LADIES:	Hits Score	Name	Year
Quadruple American	356 — 2316 (610, 573, 551, 582)		
		Lillian Eytel,	1956
Single American	90 — 610	Lillian Eytel,	1956
60 yards	30 — 190	Margaret Breneman,	1957
50 yards	30 — 214	Lillian Eytel,	1955
40 yards	30 — 236	Margaret Breneman,	1957
Clout (180 yds.)	30 — 136	Alice J. Smith,	1952

Flight:	Yds. Feet Ins.		
35 lb.	347 — 0 — 0	Mildred Miller,	1954
50 lb.	336 — 0 — 0	Fannie Brumble,	1956

MEN:	Hits Score	Name	Year
Quadruple American	360 — 2854 (698, 726, 694, 736)		
		Paul Eytel,	1955
Single American	90 — 736	Paul Eytel,	1955
60 yards	30 — 242	Paul Eytel,	1955
50 yards	30 — 248	Paul Eytel,	1955
40 yards	30 — 258	Paul Eytel,	1955
Clout (180 yds.)	35 — 307	Col. Francis E. Pierce,	1956

Flight:	Yds. Feet Ins.		
50 lb.	440 — 1 — 0	Col. Francis E. Pierce,	1955
65 lb.	497 — 0 — 0	Col. Francis E. Pierce,	1954
80 lb.	566 — 0 — 0	Col. Francis E. Pierce,	1955
Unlimited	554 — 0 — 0	Col. Francis E. Pierce,	1955

King's Round (Crossbows):

	Hits	Score		
King's Round-King	5	45	Paul Eytel,	1956
1st King's Man	4	36	Sydney G. Berliner,	1956
2nd King's Man	3	27	Fred Isles,	1956

Records (standing TARGET archery as of 1957) Canadian National Archery Association: Note: For the first time the Canadian champions were decided by regional tournaments in 1956. These were held at Alberta, British Columbia, Manitoba, Ontario, Quebec, and Saskatchewan provinces. The 1957 Canadian National Tournament was also a regional meet.

Junior Girls (Rounds)			Junior Boys (Rounds)		
	Score	Name		Score	Name
Jr. Canadian	761	Dianne Dickson	Jr. Canadian	956	Gary Forster
Jr. American	560	Marion Pearce	Jr. American	708	Gary Forster
120 yard Clout	258	Marion Pearce	120 yard Clout	282	Gary Forster

Ladies (Rounds)	Score	Name	Men's (Rounds)	Score	Name
Canadian	811	Helen Dickson	York	752	Reg. W. Hill
American	658	Helen Dickson	American	710	J. Macdonald
National	487	Helen Dickson	Canadian	872	Herb Erickson
Columbia	582	Helen Dickson	180 yard Clout	270	Andy Pyk
120 yard Clout	278	Kay Pavelick	200 yards Battle		
			Clout	221	Arnold Glennie

Flight (open)	Distance	Name
Junior Girls	327 yds., 1 ft., 5 ins.	Edna Markham
Junior Boys	304 yds.	Robert Fleet
Ladies	356 yds.	Marge Albert
Men	493 yds.	Herbert Albert

Records (standing FIELD archery) Canadian National Archery Association:

Junior Girls	Score	Name	Ladies	Score	Name
(Free Style Division) Rounds:			(Free Style Division) Rounds:		
Field 56 targets	335	Dianne Dickson	Field 56 targets	615	Betty McKeown
Broadhead 56 targets	540	Carol Dunsdon	Broadhead 56 targets	835	Betty McKeown
(Instinctive Division) Rounds:			(Instinctive Division) Rounds:		
Field 56 targets	207	Edna Markham	Field 56 targets	356	Iris Carter
Broadhead 56 targets	430	Edna Markham	Broadhead 56 targets	550	Iris Carter
Junior Boys			Men's		
(Free Style) Rounds:			(Free Style Division) Rounds:		
Field 56 targets	479	Don Harris	Field 56 targets	825	Harold Prenter
Broadhead 56 targets	835	Don Harris	Broadhead 56 targets	945	Arnold Glennie
(Instinctive) Rounds:			(Instinctive Division) Rounds:		
Field 56 targets	520	Ari Makie	Field 56 targets	698	Henry Hanson
Broadhead 56 targets	695	Ted Kirk	Broadhead 56 targets	805	Herman Walter

Note: In Canada the Men's division used broadheads in the 1956 National tournament, but the Ladies and Juniors used field arrows and their broadhead round was called the Hunters' round.

FITA WORLD TARGET ARCHERY RECORDS

There were entrants from 12 competing nations in this 1957 tournament held at Dynamo Stadium, Prague, Czechoslovakia. This was the first time that the new FITA round was shot at a World Championship Tournament. Americans won all events.

Single FITA Round—Individual Records

LADIES:			GENTLEMEN:		
Distance	*Name*	*Score*	*Distance*	*Name*	*Score*
70 meters	Ann Clark	236	90 meters	Joe Fries	249
60 meters	Carole Meinhart	309	70 meters	Sylvester Chessman	294
50 meters	Betty Schmidt	258	50 meters	O. K. Smathers	290
30 meters	Carole Meinhart	321	30 meters	Joe Fries	329
Aggregate	Carole Meinhart	1099	Aggregate	Joe Fries	1148

Double FITA Round—Individual Records

LADIES:			GENTLEMEN:		
Distance	*Name*	*Score*	*Distance*	*Name*	*Score*
70 meters	Ann Clark	462	90 meters	O. K. Smathers	446
60 meters	Carole Meinhart	574	70 meters	Joe Fries	571
50 meters	Carole Meinhart	495	50 meters	O. K. Smathers	579
30 meters	Carole Meinhart	613	30 meters	Joe Fries	657
Aggregate	Carole Meinhart	2120	Aggregate	O. K. Smathers	2231

Team Record—Single FITA Round

LADIES:		Aggregate	GENTLEMEN:		Aggregate
Name	*Score*	*Total*	*Name*	*Score*	*Total*
Carole Meinhart	1099		Joe Fries	1148	
Ann Clark	1087		O. K. Smathers	1125	
Betty Schmidt	1003	3189	Sylvester Chessman	1056	3329

Team Record—Double FITA Round

LADIES:		Aggregate	GENTLEMEN:		Aggregate
Name	*Score*	*Total*	*Name*	*Score*	*Total*
Carole Meinhart	2120		O. K. Smathers	2231	
Ann Clark	2080		Joe Fries	2221	
Betty Schmidt	1987	6187	Sylvester Chessman	2139	6591

Recurved Bow: A bow which has tip ends made with a reverse bend, either by process of steaming and bending over a form, or by laminating several bow components on a bow laminating form of the recurve design. Its purpose is to have a bow of longer length for a smoothness of draw, but with the snappy fast action of a shorter bow.

Recurved bows are divided into two basic types which are: (1) Working recurves, or those whose tip ends actually partially unbend as the bow is drawn, and (2) Non-working recurves or those with ends which are so constructed that they do not bend to any noticeable degree. The working recurve is the favorite bow of these two types. (*See* "Bow Types.")

Reel, Bow: A bow reel has the same function as a regular spinning fish reel. The reel holds a fishing line and allows the line to feed freely from its spool upon the release of the fishing arrow.

The bow reel with its line is usually taped to the back of the bow limb; the free end of the line is threaded through a small hole at the nock end of the arrow and is drawn forward to the front end of the arrow where it is then attached directly to the fishing head. When a fishing arrow is drawn upon a bow which is equipped with a bow reel, and released, the line will be freely drawn from the reel until it strikes a fish; from then on the fish is drawn back to the archer-fisher by rewinding the line onto the reel. There are a great many designs of bow reels in use today, one of which is shown here. (*See* "Fishing, Bow and Arrow.")

Reflexed Bow: A reflexed bow is one that has limbs which are either by designed construction or naturally into a reverse bend. Reflexed bows are not usually as smooth to shoot as are those whose limbs are constructed into a slight "follow the string" or "set" design. Reflexed bows are sometimes very rough on strings; i.e., a reflexed bow tends to break a string more often than a bow which is not reflexed due to the limbs trying to return to their complete reverse bend. (*See* "Naturally Reflexed," and "Bow Types.")

Release: An archer's release is the term used to define the moment at which the archer allows the bowstring and the arrow to leave the string hand. The release is further explained as follows: "The release is not what an archer does, but what he stops doing." That is, the archer merely relaxes the fingers and quits holding the string. The release will become more effective if executed in a sharp smooth crisp manner. This requires practice.

Release Types: There are other methods of string releases in archery than by the relaxation of the fingers which may have drawn the string. These are as follows: (A) The mechanical release; one which has mechanically moving parts such as the trigger mechanism in a crossbow. This is called a "mousetrap" by many archers. (B) There is another type which is known as the "bowlock" which is shaped to fit the palm of the hand and the fingers which hold it into the hand. A small hook impression on the side of this device is held behind the string as the string and the arrow are drawn. The string and the arrow are held into place by a light pressure of the thumb. Upon the release of thumb pressure the string is then free and goes into motion, thus taking the arrow with it. The nock of the arrow is placed immediately above the "bowlock" hook. Many observers believe that Frank Eicholtz of San Diego was the first to use this shooting device. (C) The "thumb ring" was a heavy ring which was worn on the thumb of the hand which drew the bowstring and the arrow. The thumb ring had the same basic function as the "bow lock" in so far as the string was held behind the ring by pressure of the thumb against the side of the index finger; when this pressure was released, the string would slip over or pass along side of the ring into motion. One should be sure that any shooting device they may plan to use will be acceptable to the tournament committee before doing so. Some clubs do not allow the use of these aids.

Reticle: A device within a viewing optic such as is explained under the heading "Game Framer." A reticle may comprise of any of the following: (1) cross hair, (2) lee dot, (3) post, (4) circles and dot, or (5) graduations.

Riser Insert: The riser insert is a block of self or laminated wood which is fashioned to give proper shape and depth to the mid-section of a laminated bow. The use of the riser insert enables a person to make a bow with considerably less waste as to the amount of stock necessary than is the case of the self bow stave.

Robin Hood: Legendary in history, he is believed to have been the greatest of yeomen; to have led a band of Merry Outlaws famous for their feats of robbing the rich and giving to the poor. Robin Hood, according to legend, was a gracious and courageous English outlaw with headquarters in Nottinghamshire's Sherwood Forest and the forest of Barnsdale. A few of his famous friends were Little John, Will Scarlet, Friar Tuck, and Allan-a-Dale, all of whom were famed yeomen of the fourteenth century.

The attire of Robin Hood was romantic in that its colors were those of the forests in which he lived; it consisted of the peak-topped leather hat with its long pheasant feather trim, a tunic type belted blouse, tights, medium height laced boots, and, of course, his long bow and leather quiver of arrows.

Roughed Out Stave: A bow stave which has been sawn or cut to its rough shape prior to the finish work of exact tillering or fashioning of the bow. The stave may be of solid stock (self stave) or of laminated construction.

Round: A round in target archery may constitute the complete shooting of any of the many games under the heading of "Rounds, Target Archery." In field archery, a round means the shooting of a complete range of targets which may vary from fourteen to fifty-six targets. The various rounds in field archery each have a different type of target and range layout. (*See* "Rounds, Field Archery.")

Round Robin: A tournament in which each archer is matched against each of the other contestants. Some Round Robin shoots use the handicap system while others shoot completely by total scores only.

Rounds, Combined: In many clubs the day's events may be a combination of two different rounds to be shot, such as in target archery where the combination of the York Round and the American Round is very popular; while in field archery, the Field Round and the Hunters or the Big Game Round may constitute the day's complete events. In either case the combined aggregate score is usually the deciding factor. Club championships are often decided by aggregate scores of several varied events.

Rounds, Crossbow: (1) In national tournament competition a Quadruple American Round is shot from the regular distances of 60, 50 and 40 yards. The standard target face is a regular five colored face; however, it is only 24″ rather than 48″ as used by the longbowmen. Note: Crossbowmen never compete with the longbowmen, nor do they shoot in the same division. Crossbowmen do, however, abide by the N.A.A. tournament rules. (2) The King's Round is a special round shot only at National tournaments, and only by the three individuals who have scored the three highest individual American Rounds, while shooting the Quadruple American Round.

Rounds, Field Archery: The ranges for the various field rounds, etc., are outlined under part (2) of "Archery Ranges" and the rounds are outlined under "N.F.A.A. Rounds." (For other rounds, *See* "Battle Clout," "Broadhead Flight" and "Novelty Round.")

The King's Round is "a sudden death round." Only six bolts (arrows) are shot by each of the three contestants, one at each of six separate 4″ golds which are equally spaced around the blue ring of a standard 48″ target. Each gold has a one-inch black center. A hit in the gold counts nine (9) while a hit in the spot is ten (10); with no other exceptions. The first man shoots at the "twelve o'clock" gold and yields to the next, in order, who does likewise until all of the six individual golds have been shot at in a manner of clockwise rotation. The man with the highest score is named the King of Crossbowmen for the ensuing year, while the other two men are named the 1st and 2nd King's men according to their respective scores.

(3) Other rounds such as the clout round and novelty rounds may be shot in accordance with the tournament committee.

Rounds, Target Archery: Each of these rounds is fully explained under their separate headings.

(1) American round: 30 arrows from each of the following distances: 60, 50, and 40 yards.

(2) Junior American round: 30 arrows from each of the following distances: 50, 40, and 30 yards.

(3) Clout (ladies'): (A) 36 arrows from 140 yards, or (B) 36 arrows from 120 yards.

(4) Clout (men's): 36 arrows from 180 yards.

(5) Clout (Junior Boys and Intermediate Girls): 36 arrows from 120 yards.

(6) Clout (Junior Girls, Beginner Boys and Girls): 36 arrows from 80 yards.

(7) Columbia round (for ladies): 24 arrows from each of the following distances: 50, 40, and 30 yards.

(8) Junior Columbia: 24 arrows from each of the following distances: 40, 30, and 20 yards.

(9) FITA round (for ladies): 36 arrows from 70 meters, 36 arrows from 60 meters, 36 arrows from 50 meters, and 36 arrows from 30 meters. (*See* "International Rounds (revised).")

(10) FITA round (for men): 36 arrows from 90 meters, 36 arrows from 70 meters, 36 arrows from 50 meters and 36 arrows from 30 meters. (*See* "International Rounds (revised).")

(11) Hereford round (for ladies and also the required round at

National meets for Intermediate Boys): 72 arrows from 80 yards, 48 arrows from 60 yards, and 24 arrows from 50 yards.

(12) International Long Round (men): 72 arrows from 90 meters or 98.4 yards, 48 arrows from 70 meters or 76.6 yards, and 24 arrows from 50 meters or 54.7 yards. (Now obsolete; See FITA Rounds.)

(13) International Long Round (for ladies): 60 arrows from 70 meters or 76.6 yards, 48 arrows from 60 meters or 65.6 yards, and 36 arrows from 50 meters or 54.7 yards. (Now obsolete; See FITA Rounds.)

(14) The International Short Round (men and ladies): 30 arrows from 50 meters or 54.7 yards, 30 arrows from 35 meters or 38.3 yards, and 30 arrows from 25 meters or 27.3 yards. (Now obsolete; See FITA Rounds.)

(15) National Round (for ladies): 48 arrows from 60 yards, and 24 arrows from 50 yards.

(16) Team round (women and intermediate girls): 96 arrows from 50 yards.

(17) Team round (men and intermediate boys): 96 arrows from 60 yards.

(18) Team round (junior girls and boys): 96 arrows from 40 yards.

(19) Team round (beginner boys): 96 arrows from 30 yards.

(20) Team round (beginner girls): 96 arrows from 20 yards.

(21) Wand shoot (men): 36 arrows from 100 yards.

(22) Wand shoot (intermediate boys): 36 arrows from 80 yards.

(23) Wand shoot (ladies and intermediate girls): 36 arrows from 60 yards.

(24) Wand shoot (junior boys): 36 arrows from 50 yards.

(25) Wand shoot (junior girls and beginner boys): 36 arrows from 40 yards.

(26) Wand shoot (beginner girls): 36 arrows from 30 yards.

(27) The York round (men): 72 arrows from 100 yards, 48 arrows from 80 yards, and 24 arrows from 60 yards.

(28) The English York round (for men): In this round, which is an English custom, the targets are located on both ends of the field. Shoot three arrows alternately from each end of the 100-yard field twelve times, which totals 72 arrows; shoot three arrows alternately from each end of the 80-yard field eight times,

which totals 48 arrows; shoot three arrows alternately from each end of the 60-yard field four times, which totals 24 arrows.

(*See also* "Olympic Round and Chicago Round" in Olympic Bowman League [O.B.L.] and "Games, Archery.")

Rules and Infractions: Both national associations, the N.A.A. and the N.F.A.A., have set rules of infractions and each association enforces these rules for the protection of both the archers and the spectator. Any archer who has been given a second warning in regard to infractions of the tournament rules may be expelled from the shoot upon the decision of the tournament officials if a third infraction is in evidence.

Rules of Order: Most clubs like to carry on their regular and special meetings with a certain degree of decorum; therefore, it is not unusual that a book containing rules of order is purchased and adopted. The book "Roberts Rules of Order" seems to be an accepted one by most clubs as it is very complete and seems to cover all legal aspects of what is right or wrong in any kind of social or formal meeting.

Rules of Safety and Things to Remember:

(1) Never point a bow or a crossbow at a person; either one can be as lethal as a gun.

(2) Never shoot your arrow until you are very certain that no one is near or behind your target. Do not allow a person to stand in front of you while you are shooting, even if the person seems a safe distance from you.

(3) Do not nock an arrow until you are certain that it is safe to do so.

(4) Remember that when shooting in a tournament double or repeated blasts on the field captain's whistle means to stop shooting immediately.

(5) Never shoot an arrow straight up into the air! One never knows exactly where that arrow will fall and a critical injury could easily be the result!

(6) A broken or cracked wood arrow should be discarded permanently to avoid a possible injury later.

(7) Never draw a bow without the arrow for which it was intended to be used, unless of the same length. Never draw another person's bow without his permission. Remember, a bow that is overdrawn is easily broken.

(8) Never shoot broadhead arrows on a target archery range unless the range is specifically designed for hunting practice.

(9) Always make it a practice to use sound judgment and good sense when you are armed with a bow and arrow. An accident can happen so easily and be costly to all concerned.

(10) Never look for a lost arrow behind an unattended target. Always leave one archer or, to say the least, stand a bow up in front of the target.

(11) In field archery always follow the paths on the range and never cross a shooting lane; an arrow may be on its way to the target and you may be seriously hurt.

(12) Always heed the instructions of the field captain. Remember the instructions are for your safety and enjoyment.

(13) As a spectator, never handle the equipment on the ranges! Good equipment is costly and easily broken when in the hands of one who does not know how to handle it.

(14) Always be a good sport on the range. Remember some archers do not appreciate a lot of chatter while they are shooting and in many cases you will find that you yourself will shoot a better round if you tend more to the business of shooting!

(15) Above all, be fair and square on the range! Archery is too old a sport and like life itself, we are here too short a time to abuse it!

Saddle Handle Grip: This is a term used to explain the present day shape of bow handles which is more of a form fit shape than those of a few years back. The "saddle handle grip" dips in considerably immediately below the upper end of the handle and on the inside of the handle. This recent improvement allows the bow hand to seat comfortably into the shape of the handle in a saddle like manner. (*See* "Handle Types.")

Sagittarius: The zodiacal constellation of the archer; hence the ninth sign of the zodiac which the sun enters on or about November 22. A mythical centaur with a drawn bow. (*See* "Centaur.")

Sagittary: Pertains to arrows, as those used by an archer.

Sagittate: Shaped like an arrowhead.

Sapwood: The layer of wood immediately under the bark of a tree. Yew wood bows and a few osage orange bows were typical of the better bows which were constructed with a thin layer of sapwood left on the back of the bow. This is to protect the heartwood from breakage on the back of a bow; however, in the case of the osage orange bow, sapwood is seldom, if ever, necessary and in most cases an osage bow has more cast if the sapwood is completely eliminated.

Saxton Pope: One of archery's all-time greats! Dr. Pope, author of the archery classic *Hunting with the Bow and Arrow,* was one of North America's first outstanding Bow Hunters. Teamed with Art Young, for whom the Big Game award is in memoriam, Dr. Pope made many memorable hunting trips. Archers shall forever after hold in reverence the memory of these two great sportsmen.

Scales, Arrow: Any sensitive or delicate scale capable of extremely accurate weighing of arrow shafts, etc. The scales which are graduated with avoirdupois method of graduations are the most commonly used scales for archery today.

Scales, Bow: Any common hook scale which is capable of fairly accurate readings to two hundred pounds can be used to check a bow's draw weight for any given length of arrow. One must understand that to obtain the accurate drawing weight of a bow the bow must be drawn to the given length of the arrow with a hook scale, at which time the scale is read.

Score: To make an actual hit on a chosen target. The combined total of any or all subtotals of one's shooting. (*See* Aggregate Scores.)

Score Card: Most archery clubs have a sheet or card which is ruled or printed with all necessary lines and columns for shooting any of the particular rounds which are outlined within this book. It is to one's advantage to keep a record of his scores. By doing so, an archer is then in actual competition with himself and will spend a great deal of time in improvement.

Among the entries which appear on a score card are: (1) the archer's name and address, (2) the name of the round or rounds to be shot, (3) itemization of the arrow hits, (4) the number of hits per target, (5) the score for each end or target (depending upon whether the round is target or field archery), (6) the total

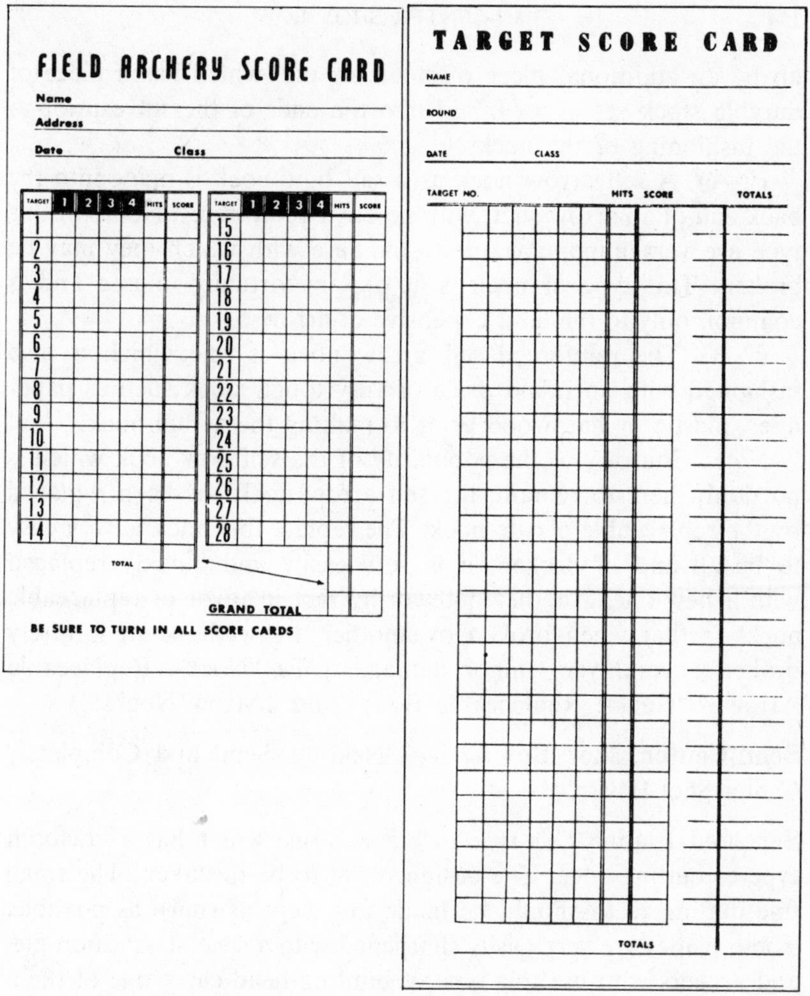

FIELD ARCHERY SCORE CARD

Name

Address

Date   Class

TARGET	1	2	3	4	HITS	SCORE	TARGET	1	2	3	4	HITS	SCORE
1							15						
2							16						
3							17						
4							18						
5							19						
6							20						
7							21						
8							22						
9							23						
10							24						
11							25						
12							26						
13							27						
14							28						

TOTAL

GRAND TOTAL

BE SURE TO TURN IN ALL SCORE CARDS

TARGET SCORE CARD

NAME

ROUND

DATE   CLASS

TARGET NO.   HITS SCORE   TOTALS

TOTALS

Figs. 23 and 24.—*These two scoring cards, typical of those explained, are available through the archery dealers.*

of all sub-totals for any round, (7) the grand total of the day's shoot, if more than one round has been shot.

Self Arrow: (*See* "Arrow Shaft.")

Self Nocks: Self nocks are divided into two types which are as follows: (1) Absolutely self, or (2) reinforced self. Both of these types are adaptable to either or both, bows and arrows.

(1-A) A self bow nock is one which is fashioned into the tip end of a bow stave without additional reinforcement.

(1-B) A reinforced self bow nock is one which is either backed up by an additional piece of stock, or one which has a piece of durable stock set in, or inlaid into the ends of the stave prior to the fashioning of the nocks.

(2-A) A self arrow nock as a self bow nock is made into the back end of an arrow shaft with no other reinforcing. Nocks of this type are very unpopular due to the ease with which they may be broken. This type of nock is at present virtually unused and is common only to the least expensive of arrows.

(2-B) The reinforced self arrow nock is one which is also fashioned with an inlaid piece of very tough stock such as paper fiber, plastic or hardwood prior to making the actual nock.

Note: Contrary to the popularity of the self bow nock which is no doubt here to remain, the self arrow nock has been replaced by the replaceable plastic nock. The replaceable nock is very easy to install and, if broken, it is very easily and quickly replaced with a new one. Another noteworthy fact in favor of replaceable nocks is that when broken by another arrow the shaft is rarely broken beyond very minor damage. (*See* "Nocks, Replaceable Arrow," "Nocks, Replaceable Bow," and "Arrow Nocks.")

Semi-Center Shot Bow: (*See* "Near or Semi and Completely Center Shot Bows.")

Serrated Blade: This type of blade is one which has a sawtooth type of cutting edge. The design is not to be mistaken. The small fine cutting teeth should be made and kept as sharp as possible. These blades are very easily sharpened with a special serration file, and archers who use this type of hunting head carry one of these files with them as part of their necessary equipment. (*See* "Razor Sharp Hunting Heads," "Trombin," and "Anti-coagulant.")

Serving: A protective wrapping of thread applied to the center portion of a bowstring. The serving is very important to eliminate wear to the bow string at this point. Caution: At any time that a spiral appears on the surface of a serving the string should be replaced immediately as this is the "telltale" sign of a broken strand of thread under the serving. A string with a broken strand is not considered safe to use.

Serving Tool: A small tool which incorporates either a bobbin filled with heavy thread, or a complete spool of thread which is so designed that it will rotate about the bowstring and apply a smooth wrapping around the string; the purpose of which is to eliminate wear by the added thread covering.

Sextuple American Round: The shooting of six regular American rounds which is usual in a National tournament for the Sextuple American Division only.

Shaft Support: An adjustable device with a "V" type groove on its upper surface which is used for the purpose of aligning an arrow shaft to a point cutting tool or sanding disc. This jigg is for shop production work.

Shooting Area: In target archery a space of not less than six feet behind a shooting line. Spectators should stay out of this area.

Shooting an End in National Target Competition: (1) If only three archers are on a target, the Target Captain shall shoot three arrows and yield his place to his target mates. The mates shall shoot their first three arrows and yield their place again to the first shooter, who shall then shoot his three remaining arrows and again yield his place to the target mates who shall shoot their remaining three arrows. (2) If four or more archers are on the same target, the Target Captain and one or two others (usually those having the higher scores) may shoot their first three arrows, yield to their target mates while they shoot their first three arrows. The target mates then yield their places to the first archers who must then shoot their remaining three arrows and again yield their places for the second group to finish shooting their remaining three arrows.

(3) If threatening weather or darkness is in evidence, the officials of the tournament may decide that the archers may shoot all six arrows before yielding their places to their target mates, or they may request that all archers shoot simultaneously.

Shooting Glove: This is an accessory necessary to protect the fingers from bowstring burn and is worn as a regular glove would be on the hand which draws and releases the bow string. (*See* "Tab.")

Shooting Line: The line, or lines, marked on the ground parallel to the line of targets and which is perpendicular to the shooting lanes of an archery range. In target archery the shooters should straddle the shooting line. In field archery the archers must stand behind the shooting lines.

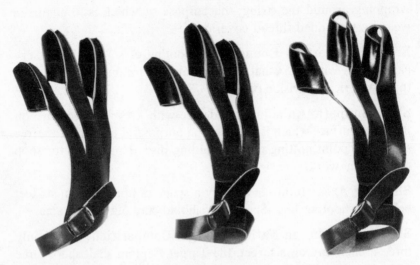

Three popular types of shooting gloves made by the King Sport-Line Co. Two of these gloves have an elastic insert in the back but each has different types of tips. The other glove has a form-fitting back with open glove tips. (Photo courtesy of King Sport-Line.)

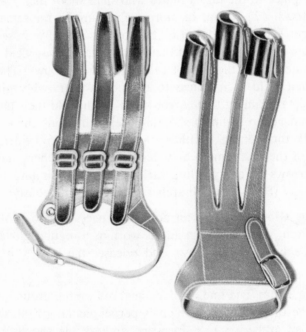

Additional types of the many popular types of shooting gloves. One of these gloves is adjustable to the length of the hand by means of the individual buckles. (Photo courtesy of Warrior Manufacturing Co.)

Sight, Bow: There are many versions of bow sights which are adaptable to archery bows. Many of these sights are popular with both target and field archers. Some have peep holes, others have pin type aim indicators, while others have either ground glass lenses or prisms for distance. Regardless of the type, most archers will shoot a better score by using a sight than they will be capable of shooting by instinct. This has been proven by the top scores

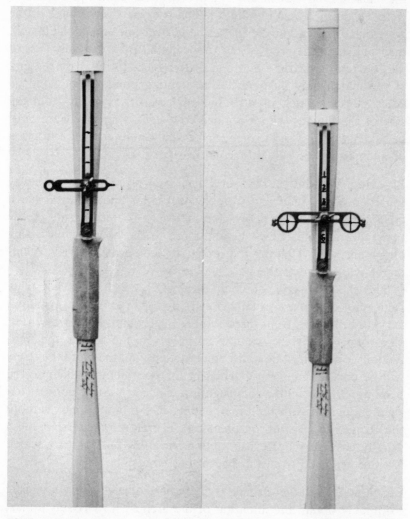

Plain and prism lenses and the pin- and peep-hole types of aiming bars. The prism lens is used for light weight bows at the longer distances, while the other types are merely a matter of choice for distances to approximately 80 yards.

which are shot by the "free style" archers (with sights) in comparison to top scores shot by the instinctive archers in national competition.

Sight, Bow (temporary): On occasion a person will find that he has left his bow sight home, or perhaps he may not even own one, which leads up to the temporary sight. A match stick held across the back of a bow by means of a short rubber band will work very well. To do this, merely hold a match stick across the back of the bow, place one end of the rubber band over one end of the match, then pull the other end of the rubber band over the belly side of the bow and over the other end of the stick. In this case the end of the match may be used as the sighting pointer. For windage adjustment the stick may be moved inwardly or away from the side of the bow as with a regular bow sight. Caution: Care must be taken with this sight since even a slight bump of but a fraction of an inch may result in a complete miss.

Sighting Windows: This term has been given to the cut away space on Near, Semi and Completely Center Shot bows. It has a dual purpose: (1) it allows the arrow to pass alongside of the upper portion of a bow's handle more to the bow's actual string alignment; (2) it allows the archer to have a better view of his target while aiming the bow and arrow.

The modern types of composite bows which have complete centershot design are usually constructed with long sight windows varying in lengths from three to nine inches above the arrow rest. The longer the sight window is, however, the longer the mid-section or riser must be to accommodate it, and the more the stress will be on the remaining portion of the bow's limbs which do the bending. A bow with a long sighting window must be constructed rigid enough to withstand the bending of the bow's limbs without the danger of twisting or breaking. Therefore, Centershot bows usually have very deep riser sections to allow for the stock which is to be removed from the side of the bow.

Signals: Most target or field archery field officials carry a whistle to quickly obtain the attention of the archers. (1) A single blast is to begin or to cease shooting as applicable. (2) Continued blasts are a signal to cease shooting immediately and give attention to the officials.

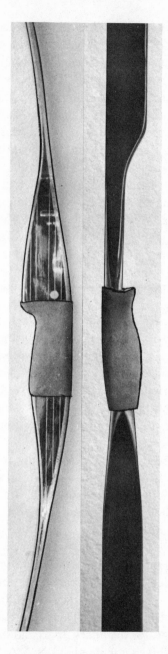

The sighting window (side and belly views) of a completely centershot bow. This bow, a deep D-flex, is one which has its riser equally centered within the belly and back of the bow.

Sinew: Heel and/or loin tendons from deer or other animals, when dried, shredded and degreased, are then called sinew. Sinew is dampened and glued to the back of a bow with either animal glue or Casco water-resistant glue. The sinew must be put on in closely laid layers and in an overlapping manner. When an entire sinew backing has been applied, a one-inch gauze bandage should be wrapped around the bow from handle toward the tip ends; first lightly in one direction and then wrap another lightly in the opposite direction, also starting at the handle.

A sinew backing should be laid completely through the entire length of the bow stave. Aside from the composite bows made by the Turkish archers which were backed with sinew, it was also used in early American days by the Indians for their bowstrings. This kind of a string, of course, has given way to the linen or dacron string; while the sinew backings have given way to the more efficient, and far more easily applied, fiberglas backings.

Six-Golds Pins: These awards are given to target archers of both the longbow and crossbow divisions, who are affiliated with the N.A.A., for shooting a perfect end, or six consecutive arrows, into the bull's-eye in any one end.

All six-golds tournaments must be approved prior to the day of the shoot to be allowable for six-golds pin awards. These shooting days may, however, be a regular club shooting day or they may be days held open as special events days.

All six-golds scores must be witnessed by the field captain and, because all six-golds tournaments require double scoring, both cards must be properly filled out with the archer's full name, the round which was shot, the date, and mailed to the national secretary for approval and the award.

The Six-Golds Pin for the N.A.A. Longbow division is a miniature five-colored target which is $15/32$nd of an inch in diameter with one gold arrow which appears to partially protrude from opposite sides; the bull's-eye or gold has six small black dots arranged therein to represent six arrows. These pins are awarded free of charge by the N.A.A. for distances up to and including sixty yards. A special award is given for qualified N.A.A. six-golds shot from eighty yards. This distinction is shared by only four archers in the United States; they are Herb Taylor of Sacramento, California, first to receive this award; William Glackin, past N.A.A. men's

National Champion, Joe Fries, Los Angeles, the 1955, 1956, and 1957 National Champion, and Sylvester Chessman of Cleveland. The latter two archers accomplished this feat in the same end; however, on seperate targets, in the 1955 National Tournament at Oxford, Ohio. (*See* "Range Buttons.")

The pin for the National Company of Crossbowmen is silver with silver arrows. Another distinction between these two pins is that the pin for the National Company of Crossbowmen is so designed that pendant bars may be attached showing the ranges from which the six golds were shot. These awards are given out only upon notification by the N.A.A. secretary to the secretary of the N.C.C.

Skirt: The skirt of a target is that part which is outside of the line of the lowest scoring circle.

Slat Tapering Jigg: A jigg used by bowyers for the purpose of tapering a bow lamination. These jiggs are many in design and operation. Some are made for use with the circular saw while others are made to run through a power sander with the slat. The taper of course is dependent upon the type of bow to be made.

Smooth drawing: The ease with which a bow may be drawn to the full length of an arrow without apparent "stacking of weight." A quality which deems a bow "smooth" or one which "stacks."

Sons of Liberty Bowl: Although this bowl remains in the custody of the N.F.A.A., the name of each year's Men's National Champion is attached thereto on a silver disc which hangs from the rim of the bowl.

The bowl, a sterling silver replica of the Paul Revere Bowl, approximately eight inches high and twelve inches in diameter, is inscribed "National Field Archery Association Championship Bowl. Gift of the Archers of Michigan, 1946."

Sox: A bow sox is a tubular piece of cloth, usually wool jersey, made to snugly fit the limbs of a bow. (1) A bow sox is used to eliminate light reflections from a bow by archery hunters. (2) A bow sox is a protection to a bow from scratches and bumps, either of which are not conducive to a well-kept piece of equipment.

Space Aiming: (*See* "Instinctive or Space Aiming.")

Speed of a Bow: (*See* "Cast of a Bow.")

Spent Arrow: An arrow which has reached its maximum velocity and is then falling off in its trajectory to the target; exhausted of effectiveness.

Spine, Arrow: The spine of an arrow shaft has reference to its stiffness, either singularly or in relation to another, or other shafts. Spine is termed low, medium, or high. The latter, in terms of archery, means very stiff in relation to the shaft diameter. (*See* "Matched Shafts.")

Spine Tester: A device used to check arrow shafts for their relative stiffness. There are direct reading and calculated dial types; the use of either type is far better than none at all. Arrow shafts can be very roughly spine checked by hand but one must be familiar with this method or his time will be wasted.

Spine Testing: The spine of an arrow is tested by means of hanging a weight (usually two pounds) onto the shaft, after first supporting it by both of its ends. (1) The spine reading will be consistent *only* if it is straight. (2) The spine should be checked with the grain layers on edge. Note: There are exceptions to part two, which are (a) a compressed cedar shaft should be tested for spine with its grain layers horizontal to the table while, (b) a dural (aluminum alloyed), or a glass shaft have no specific grain to allow for.

Splicing Jigg: A jigged vice used by a bowyer to hold a billet while a splice is being sawed. Billets are usually quite irregular in shape and are rarely, if ever, square. Therefore the splicing jigg is very helpful to one who intends to make a bow from spliced billets.

Spotting Aids: The N.A.A. has the following rules for the use of spotting aids: (1) While in the act of shooting his three successive arrows, or if shooting six arrows consecutively, an archer may not leave the shooting line to use a spotting scope or aid. (2) Archers may use spotting aids only after retiring from the shooting line, or while their target mates are in the process of shooting.

Stacked Type Bow: This term has reference to the English long bow design where the limbs are narrow and deep in cross sectional shape. The belly side of a stacked type of bow was usually rounded to a half round shape, while the sides were at right angles to the general shape of the back of the bow. Bows of this type have lost practically all favorable recognition within the past twenty years due to the tedious job of tillering them to proper bend and string alignment. Note: Flat backed and flat bellied bows are very fast and easily tillered, comparatively speaking.

Stacking on the Draw: A bow which is referred to as one which "stacks on the draw" is one which has a noticeable uneven buildup of its draw weight near to the end of the arrow; i.e., some bows will have a very uniform increase in inch per inch draw to an arrow. For example, let us say a bow draws 30 pounds at 24", 32½ pounds at 25" and 35½ pounds at 26". This bow would be smooth to draw. A second bow, same design, may draw 30 pounds at 24", 34 pounds at 25" and then at 26" it may have a drawing weight of 40 pounds pull. This bow, as is evident, would be one with apparent stacking, and would also be one which would be hard to shoot constantly well. (*See* "Smooth Drawing.")

Stalking (of game): To approach, follow or pursue game under cover or by stealth. Hunting archers must learn to overcome or conquer all of the mysteries of the woods to stalk game properly. The average big game shot with bow and arrow is made from approximately thirty-five yards, and to approach wildlife of any kind and reach a distance this short without being seen or heard requires considerable skill to achieve. To stalk game does not necessarily mean that there is intent to kill it; stalking may be done as practice, provided no actual shot is made. This is as important as is practice shooting on an archery range. (*See* "Bowman Hunter," "Hunting Archery," "Lure Calls," and "Lure Scents.")

Stance: An archer's posture while shooting a bow and arrow. Good stance requires the following points: (1) Stand relaxed and comfortably erect. (2) Feet should be spaced a comfortable distance apart, usually between 8 and 14 inches apart, depending upon the individual. (3) Stand straddle the shooting line, body facing the side lines but with the head facing the target.* (4) Stand approximately 18 inches away from either of the lane lines *unless directed to do otherwise.* (5) Upon completion of shooting

---

* In N.F.A.A. field archery practice and Tournaments, the archer must stand behind all shooting lines or stakes.

an end always step back from the shooting line and not forward of it.

Stretching Jigg: A special jigg used by bowstring makers to remove the stretch from a bowstring and also to hold the string under tension while the center serving is applied. A string may be placed on a bow for the application of the center serving if a jigg of this type is not available for use. These jiggs are used more for the production string maker than the individual archer who makes an occasional bowstring for personal use.

String Grooves: A string groove is the continuation of the bow nock along the belly side of a recurved bow. These grooves usually extend to a point where the string loses its contact with the belly and the beginning of the curved tip ends.

String Server: (*See* "Serving Tool.")

Strung Bow: Also, a bow which has been braced for shooting. A bow which is held into a bent curve by a bowstring attached to its two nock ends. Note: A bow should be unstrung after use and never be laid up prior to unstringing.

Stump Shooter: A term used to signify a field archer. (*See* "The Old Stump.")

Tab: A tab is a piece of flat leather fashioned to wear on the inside of the string hand as a protection from "string burn" to the fingers. (*See* "Finger Tabs.") A tab will serve the same purpose as that of the shooting glove and in many cases preferred because of the freedom it affords to the fingers.

Tackle: Archery equipment in general, which includes all items necessary to make up an archer's complete shooting and storage equipment; i.e., his bow, arrows, strings, quivers, armguard, glove or tab, tackle storage case, etc.

Archery tackle is divided into the following classes: (a) target, (b) hunting, (c) flight shooting, (d) fishing, and (e) archery golf, which requires both target and flight equipment.

Tackle Area (also called bench area): An area which is immediately behind the shooting area. In most clubs the bench and shooting area requirements are not less than six feet of space for each.

TAM (The Archer's Magazine): The official organ of the National Archery Association which keeps abreast of the news and views of target archery in general. This magazine covers local, state, regional and national target archery events.

TAM is furnished with all memberships into the National Archery Association of the United States, or it is available to individual subscribers. (*See* "Magazines, Archery.") Aside from the archery news, TAM includes a very comprehensive run down on many other items related to archery.

Target: Any object or thing that an archer deliberately aims at with intent to hit upon the release of his arrow, and not necessarily a target matt or straw butt.

Target Assignment: This decision is up to the tournament committee and may be as follows: First round—(1) alphabetically, (2) order of registration, (3) by drawing of names. Note: In no case is it permissible to allow fewer than three archers to shoot on a single target in tournament shooting. It is customary to have four archers, or more if necessary, on each target.

Target Face: A devised target, which may be of any particular design and which is for the purpose of checking one's ability to shoot consistently as aimed. Target faces vary with the rounds to be shot on them, such as target archery faces and field archery faces.

(A) A standard face for target archery is 48 inches in diameter which is spaced, colored, and valued as follows: (a) bull's-eye, gold, value 9, size 9.6 inches; red ring, value 7, size 19.2 inches; blue ring, value 5, size 28.8 inches; black ring, value 3, size 38.4 inches; white ring, value 1, size 48″. NOTE: The gold may have a black spot in the dead center not to exceed 3″; (a) three archers only, all must prefer its use; (b) four archers, three must prefer its use; (c) if five archers are on the same target, four must prefer its use.

(B) A standard target for Crossbowmen is a 24″ five-colored face in exact proportion to the 48-inch face used by the long bowmen.

(C) Field archery faces are as follows: (1) Field round: A white or gray inner circle of exactly one half of the total diameter of the target and which is surrounded by a white or black ring only. A black aiming spot not to exceed one-fourth of the diameter

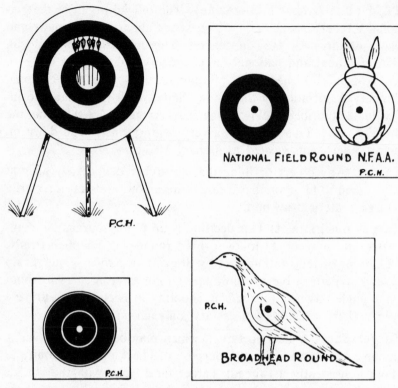

Figs. 25-28.—A. A regular target archery tripod, matt and face in black and white. B. Field archery faces. C. The Hunters round face. D. The Big Game or Broadhead round.

of the bull's-eye is used. The values of this target are as follows: entire bull's-eye area counts 5 and the entire outer circle is 3. These faces are 6 inches, 12 inches, 18 inches and 24 inches over-all. (2) The Hunters' round: this face is the same size, has all dimensions the same, and has equal scoring values to the Field round face, but this face has a white aiming center and is all black with fine white scoring lines. (3) The Big game round: these faces are life-sized animal faces with a scoring circle in the killing area as the bull's-eye while the remainder of the target is of the next lower value. Note: On this type of face the feet, lower legs, tails, horns, antlers, etc., are usually marked off as no scoring areas, and the scoring circle is invisible from shooting positions.

Target Lanes: Allotted spaces for each group which are to shoot on any particular target. The lanes are usually chalked lines on

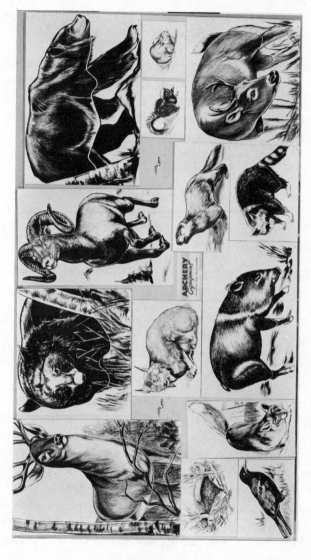

A set of life-sized targets for hunting practice and the N.F.A.A. Big Game Round. (Faces and photo are by Universal Targets)

the ground which run perpendicular to the line of target faces and to the shooting lines which are parallel to the line of targets. A lane for convenience of four shooters is usually near to 15 feet wide, in which case the two outer archers will stand about 18 inches inside of the lines, while the four archers are then spaced three feet apart from center to center.

Target Matts and Butts: Special provisions made as arrow back stops immediately behind the target faces. They may be factory made or straw bales supported upon special stands for this purpose. The face of a target matt or butt must lean away from the shooters not less than 12 degrees, nor more than 18 degrees.

Target Points: (*See* "Arrow Points.")

Target Range: (*See* "Archery Range.")

Target Reassignment: Archers are reassigned to targets in relation to comparative total scores for and after each round.

Target Tripod: A three-legged stand used to hang a target matt and face on.

Tassel: During the winter months some target archers may be seen wearing a large tassel made from brightly colored wool yarn. The purpose of this is to wipe moisture and damp grass from their arrows after retrieving them.

Taxus: (The botanical name for yew wood.) It is from the evergreen variety of trees and even though it resembles the texture of clear soft-grained Douglas Fir, the comparison should stop there. This wood, though light in weight, is extremely tough and springy. Its color ranges from a creamy white to a deep salmon red with a sapwood of almost white color. Its lightness of handling weight is very noticeable in comparison to other bow woods, which alone is a major reason for its being preferred to many other woods for bows. The very fast action and its smooth shooting qualities are also outstanding if the bow is properly made.

Team: A team of archers shall consist of four archers. In case a total of three shoot on a team, their three scores must compete against a complete team.

Team Rounds: (a) The ladies, junior girls, and junior boys all shoot the same team round which consists of the following: Shoot sixteen ends of six arrows each from fifty yards. In this round the contestants shoot on a standard 48-inch target, and they walk a total distance of 1620 yards to and from the targets. (B) In the gentlemen's team round sixteen ends of six arrows are shot from a distance of sixty yards. In this round the standard 48-inch target is used and the contestants will walk a total distance of 1920 yards to and from the targets. (C) The intermediate girls' and boys' team round also requires shooting sixteen ends of six arrows. This group shoots from forty yards. The total distance required to walk to and from the targets is 1280 yards. The 48-inch standard target is used. (D) The beginner girls' and boys' team round requires sixteen ends of six arrows from thirty yards. The total distance required to walk to and from the targets is 960 yards. The standard 48-inch target face is also used in this round.

Technique, Archery: The method or basic procedure with which one performs with expertness in any science. With archery, it is the manner with which an archer is capable of shooting his best score; i.e., his stance as he shoots, his bow hand grip, draw, anchor, checking or planning the shot, the release, follow through, and his general coordination during this entire period. Good technique does not always come easily, but will, in most cases, require considerable practice and a great deal of will power to singularly eliminate faults as they may appear.

Technique Correction: These important facts relative to archery technique should be remembered in all fairness to the maker of the equipment in use, whether the situation seems to involve the bow, the arrows, or the accessories. Do not blame your equipment arbitrarily since the fault may be due to your own inability to analyze your errors, and unsportsmanlike criticism may only lead to unpleasantness and poorer scores.

If your shooting has been up to your expectations and you later find that you are shooting left, right, or erratically, it should be taken for granted that *you* are doing something wrong. It is very easy to unknowingly alter the position of the bow hand on the handle in a manner which will give you right or left grouping. This seemingly unimportant error, however slight it may be, can spoil a good score in a hurry.

(1) As a check on your trouble (a) sight your bow for string alignment from both ends. This takes but a minute. No doubt you will find that the trouble lies elsewhere so (b) check your arrows for straightness and use only the ones which are straight. As to the arrow spine, they are probably the same arrows with which you shot your good scores previously. (c) The glove or tab could give you trouble if either has a deep impression, and should be replaced with new ones.

(2) Remember these ways of checking left and right shooting: (a) If the bow handle is twisted only *minutely* to the left while the release is being executed, the arrow will very likely go to the right on the target—the opposite is true if the handle is lightly twisted to the right. (b) If the nock end of the arrow is not drawn to a point exactly as is customary to your form, you can also shoot left or right hand groups, or very erratically if your anchor point is not consistently the same.

(3) If you seek help from someone to check your troubles for you, be sure that you consult a person who is sincere, a real instructor, and one who is not out to sell your equipment short for the sake of selling you something else. (Remember, in most cases a set of archery equipment which will check out as explained in step (1) is usually very capable of shooting much higher scores than the one who uses it.)

(4) There are many fine bows and arrows being made presently—most of which are capable of National Championship scores. However, one does not become a champion through the planned use of any specific make of bow, set of arrows, or accessory. One becomes a champion by becoming familiar first with the equipment to be used, by self discipline and practice, neither of which has any room for unjustly laying the blame of his errors on the equipment.

Telescoping Arrows: Any arrow which may strike the nock end of another arrow already in the target, and penetrate itself in a telescoping manner into that arrow, will be counted the same value as the arrow which is actually in the target, even though the telescoping arrow may not reach the target.

Temperature and its Effect on Archery Equipment: A bow's drawing weight is increased by temperatures which are below normal and the bow weight will decrease to a slight degree when shooting on a hot day. The same is true of the bow's cast; on a cold day a bow will shoot somewhat faster than at normal temperature and on a hot day that same bow will appear to have lost some of its "get up and go," so to speak. Caution: (1) It is not safe to shoot a bow in extremely cold weather as the moisture within the wood cells will freeze and as this moisture is somewhat of a lubricant to the cells and wood fibres it may be the very reason that the bow may "blow up." (2) Flexing a bow is the same as warming up a car or anything else which has moving parts. It aids the lubrication system and creates longer life. (3) Never leave a bow strung up in a car where the hot sun's rays can be directly on it. This can cause the adhesive which holds the facing on the bow to let loose and be the direct cause of the facing breaking loose from the bow.

Templates (archery): Patterns used by artisans, as a bowyer or fletcher, or both. Some of these templates are riser insert templates, string layouts, splice templates, feather trimmer wire shapes, and cresting templates.

Tennon: The front end of an arrow shaft where it is either reduced in size to fit a parallel pile or point, or the tapered end which is to be put into a point with a tapered ferrule. The same applies to nocks with a parallel hole and nocks with tapered holes. The portion of the shaft which is fit into either is also a tennon.

Tennon Tool: A hand operated or motor driven cutter which is used to remove the stock necessary to install arrow nocks or points. Since both are made with either a parallel or tapered hole, there are special tools adaptable to either job. The hand operated tools are very fine for the archer's repair kit while in the field, since one never knows when he may have to re-tennon a shaft for a new nock or point. These tools are not intended for use on glass arrow shafts. Tools for that purpose require special cutters. (*See* "Arrow Pile" and "Arrow Points.")

The National Archery Association (of America): (*See* "Associations, National.")

The National Field Archery Association (of America): (*See* "Associations, National.")

The Old Stump: The official emblem of the National Field Archery Association, adopted by the association in 1941. The stump emblem has an arrow sticking out of it which is to be symbolic of archers in the field, or as field archers are often called, "Stump Shooters." (*See* "Assns. Natl." Part (2).)

Thompson Medal of Honor, The J. Maurice: The highest award it is possible for one to attain in target archery. (*See* "Associations, National," under N.A.A.)

The highest award attainable in the National Archery Association. This medal is gold in color, approximately 2" in diameter and is over ⅛" thick.

Threads (common to Archery): For many years pure Irish linen thread was the only wise choice due to its strength and lack of stretching qualities. In the past few years new synthetic threads have been developed which are far superior. Some of these threads are Fortisan and Heat stretched Dacron. Both of these threads are lower in cost and superior in qualities for bow strings than linen.

Thrombin: A substance which *by shocking injury to skin tissue* interacts with fibernogen, thus inducing fiberin ferment, or coagulable lymph; in turn, this reaction causes the immediate action of coagulation or clotting of the shed blood. There has been considerable comment about using "razor sharp" blades, but with little spoken in regard to one of the important basic reasons of what induces hemorrhage and quick kills. It is not very often that a dull blade does this! The definition of Thrombin will tend to bring out the importance of the "razor sharp" blade. It has less shocking injury than a dull blade; therefore, less fiberin ferment would be in immediate action and little if any coagulable lymph; hence no coagulation and more hemorrhage. Blades should be kept sharp. (*See* "Razor Sharp Hunting Heads," and "Serrated Blade.")

Ties and how they are decided in N.F.A.A. Field Tournaments: Article VII, Revised 9th Edition of the N.F.A.A. Official Handbook—*Scoring* part (8): Ties may be shot off on the first three targets or decided in accordance with the mail tournament rules; i.e., by the best score on 28 targets; if still tied, by the person who has the best score on either of the 14 target units.

Ties and how they are decided in target archery: Depending upon the round, or rounds, which is to be decided upon the act of breaking a tie is at times quite a drawn-out procedure. The method may include the following: (1) The highest total of a double round; (2) the highest of either single round; (3) the highest totals of the longest distance shot in the rounds; (4) the highest total of the next longest distance, etc. If the tie still exists, (5) the greatest number of 9's in the combined rounds, or the 7's, or the 5's, etc. If the tie may still exist, the last and deciding factor will require the checking of (6) the greatest number of perfect ends. If a tie still exists, the contestants are considered truly tied and this is then set down in the records and the report of the scores.

Tie Downs: Pieces of hardwood or plastic, etc., which are used for the specific purpose of safely binding a facing or a backing to a bow. Tie downs are not always necessary and in many cases are applied for purely ornamental purpose.

Tiller: To tiller a bow is to work it to a point of proper bending and string alignment. At this stage of making a bow the person making the bow must proceed with the greatest of care and to the utmost of their skill.

Tiller or Prop Stick: A stick which is fashioned with several notches cut into one of its edges and a notch on each of its ends, one of which is to set over the bow handle and the other for the use of the complete length of the stick. This stick is used to prop a bow to different arrow lengths to study the curvature of its limbs while the tillering is in process. A prop stick should be made from hardwood such as ash, hickory or birch for safety.

Tillering Jigg: A device used by bowyers which enables them to gauge an exact taper to a bow's limbs regardless of irregularities which may be on the back of the bow. This jigg is one of the most important jiggs in a bowyer's shop as a time saver on self bows and it insures proper tillering in one-third the time required to make a self bow without the jigg. The fact that this jigg may not be familiar to many of the tacklemakers is that it is the jigg which brought about the Highland Duplicating machine patented by the author. Since that time there have been several of these jiggs sold to bowyers.

"Timber": The word "timber" is used in archery in the same manner as "fore" is used in golf; i.e., it is a word of warning and means that an archer has loosed an arrow or is about to do so.

Timber Hitch: This type of knot is often referred to as a "bow knot." One end of some strings is made without a loop or eye, in which case the timber hitch is used. Strings of this type are capable of use for bows within their range of length which is usually a variation of four to six inches. (*See* Fig. 2 in nomenclature of the bowstring.)

Toe Markers: Small pegs which are placed in the ground or turf to locate the exact position of the archers' toes when they are shooting. These are used by archers who shoot with the "Point of Aim" method as it is imperative that the archers shoot from the exact same position each time. This then is the reason for the importance of the toe markers. (*See* Figs. 17-20.)

Tournament: Any group in competition as a contest. There are local club tournaments which are usually on a monthly and quarterly basis, annual state shoots for the purpose of finding the state champions, and national tournaments which are also annual events to find the overall national champions. State and national tournaments are usually held in a different location each year to give archers a more even chance to attend them occasionally.

Tournament Courtesy: In all tournaments there are a few rules which when applied affect both the contestant and his opponents; these are rules of courtesy and must not be forgotten. A few of these are as follows: (1) Be prompt to register for your tournament so no one has to wait for you to do so. (2) Be quiet while you are shooting and if you finish shooting ahead of your target mates, do not disturb them by noisy or erratic movements. (3)

Respect the club or tournament rules; they are for everyone's pleasure and protection. (4) Do not criticize your opponents' equipment under any condition, even in jest. It is no doubt the very best which he or she may be able to own. (5) If anything in the way of helpful comment is in order, be tactful in the way you present it. No one should be put out with a truly sincere attempt to aid them.

Tournament Tackle: The better of one's archery equipment; the best which is at his disposal.

Toxophilite: One who is fond of archery, but more interested in its history than as a sport.

Trajectory: The path or the curved arc which any projectile travels from its propellant or its source of kinetic energy to any given point or target. (*See* "Gravity and its Relation to Trajectory.")

Triangulation (in archery): The process of estimation of an arrow's trajectory path by a trigonometrical survey of the elements involved which include: (1) the bow's cast, (2) the weight of the arrow, (3) the estimated distance to the target, (4) the distance which the arrow is anchored below the aiming eye, climatic conditions, etc., all of which become more familiar circumstances through practice.

Trophies: Any memento significant of a victory. One of the most important gestures a club can make toward its membership, especially when awarded to archers of the lower scoring groups. (*See* "Medals, N.A.A., and "Medals, N.F.A.A.")

Turkish Recurve: The bows which were made by the Turks were of the long bow designation as we speak of bows today; i.e., not of the crossbow or arbalest group. When braced for shooting they measured between 34 to 45 inches in length, which would mean that their total lengths, following the line of the limbs, may be 37 to 48 inches respectively from nock to nock, which is actually a very short bow to draw an arrow of 24½ to 28 inches in length. Some of these bows were so severely reflexed from the handle and so recurved on their tip ends that it made them look like the letter "C," unstrung. Actually some of these bows were bent reversely as far as they were drawn for shooting, and to string a bow of this type required the advantage of a special harness arrangement known as a Kemend. This was a string or rope long enough to allow it to be placed on the bow's nocks and then it was passed behind the archer's waist while in a sitting position. In turn, by pushing the bow away from himself with his feet, the archer was then able to put the regular string on the bow.

The materials used for these bows were (1) unusually select maple for the core stock, (2) Asiatic water buffalo horn cut into workable strips for the belly of the bow, and (3) sinew, which was used for the bow backing, other than the glues which were used.

The design of the bow was a fairly small shallow mid-section or handle, which tapered off into a wide flat oval limb, which then tapered in width to approximately ¾ of an inch at its tip ends. The limb shape ahead of the curves had a cross section resembling a triangle with round corners. From this point the tips were recurved to resemble the 60-degree angle curve of our modern bows.

The appearance of these bows was greatly enhanced by being ornately decorated, and since it took a long time to make one of these bows they no doubt sold for a very attractive price. The bows which are still in existence are valued collectors' items since they have not practiced this skill for over a century. Many of these bows are over 200 years old.

Contrary to general belief, the average weights of these bows were comparable to the modern flight bows of today and ranged around 65 pounds pull. However, there were instances where these bows were known to reach 180 pounds pull.

As to the distances shot with the Turkish composite bows, interpretation of the records shows that the greatest distance attained was 972 yards and 8 inches. Other records, however, show the advancement stages as being from 400 to 810 yards.

Perhaps if the advancement of our modern bow design continues to improve and our own modern flight records continue in the future as they have in the past, and there is no reason to believe otherwise, one day our bows may exceed these outstanding distances. It seems safe to say that we are not far from this accomplishment now with a record of 774 yards which was made in 1955 by Charles Pierson in the free style class. This may have been the same style of shooting used by the Turks; i.e., using the foot bow method of shooting. (See "Flight Bow Designation.")

Source of this information was "Turkish Archery and the Composite Bow," by Paul E. Klopsteg which was published by Mr. Klopsteg.

Twenty Pin (National): This pin was first adopted in 1942 by the National Field Archery Association. Its purpose, of course, is to create shooting interest and as recognition to those archers who are in good standing for shooting a perfect score in the National Field Round on any target from 35 yards or more. Any tournament in which this pin may be an award must be on record with the N.F.A.A. prior to the shooting day to be valid. A perfect score on a standard field round face will comprise four hits within the 5 ring or the bull's-eye, and since all National tournament awards require witnesses and double scoring, both cards and the "twenty" target must be witnessed by the field captain (official) and two other contestants. These cards must be filled out and sent to the National Secretary-Treasurer. All N.F.A.A. ranges must be approved by proper officials of the N.F.A.A.

Both divisions, instinctive and free style, are eligible for the National Twenty Pin. The original pin slightly over ⅜″ inch in diameter was a miniature field target face with a gold arrow through its center.

Unlimited Class: This is a class in which flight shooters may shoot bows of any weight and all bows in these events must compete against one another.

The original Twenty Pin, adopted by the N.F.A.A. in 1942, was designed by the Northern California Field Archers; center, the present National Twenty Pin, which was adopted in 1952; right, designed by S. F. ("Stew") Foster of the Pasadena Roving Archers. The two National pins are black and white baked enamel on gold base, with gold lines, while the broadhead is of sterling silver which is deeply engraved. The original Twenty Pin is slightly over ⅜″ in diameter; the present Twenty Pin for the N.F.A.A. is 9/16″, and the Pasadena pin is ½″ high and ½″ wide at its longest dimensions.

Unilateral: Some of the fiberglas backings and facings are constructed in this manner which means from one side. In this case the woven strands appear to show from one side more so than the opposite side, which is the face.

Vane: The feathers or fletching of an arrow. Vanes are also made of molded rubber and plastic.

Velocity: The speed of an arrow in flight. Modern bows, other than those made specifically for flight shooting, shoot between 160 and 200 feet per second, dependent upon the weight of the arrow, type of fletching used, the weight of the bowstring (light or heavy), climatic conditions, and the archer's ability to shoot with good flight shooting form. In regard to flight bows and flight arrows, the same conditions prevail; however, since the materials used to make this equipment are always selected from the best of stock with the ultimate in design and quality being the paramount objective, good flight bows and arrows do exceed the speeds mentioned by a considerable margin. Our modern flight bows (not free style or foot bow but hand bows) will shoot an arrow reasonably close to 230 feet per second while the foot-type bow used in the Free Style class has an arrow velocity of nearly 280 feet per second. (*See* "Fletching," "Flight Bows," "Flight Bow Designation," and "Flight Bow Weight Classes, N.A.A. 1955.")

Wand Shooting: Shooting at a vertical soft wood slat two inches wide and long enough that it can be securely stuck into the ground with six feet exposed. Six ends of 6 arrows consisting of 36 totai shall be shot in competition. Rules of target archery apply to this round: (A) All arrows sticking into the wand are counted as hits. (B) All rebounds are counted as hits if witnessed by the official witness. Note: Each wand shall have an official spotting witness who must immediately report the rebound to the score keepers. (C) No arrow which lies over one arrow length beyond the wand can be scored.

   (1) The Men's wand round requires the shooting of 36 arrows from 100 yards.

   (2) The Intermediate boys' wand round: 36 arrows from 80 yards.

   (3) The ladies' and Intermediate girls' wand round: 36 arrows from 60 yards.

(4) Junior boys' wand round: 36 arrows from 50 yards.

(5) Junior girls' and beginner boys' wand round: 36 arrows from 40 yards.

(6) Beginner girls' wand round: 36 arrows from 30 yards.

Warped Tips: If a bow's tip ends or the bow limb should be somewhat warped or out of alignment with the bowstring, one will find that he will have difficulty to a varied degree, depending upon the amount of warp, in shooting this bow where he aims it. That is, when a warped bow is drawn the limbs or the tip ends rarely if ever pull into alignment, but they will tend to go farther from alignment which will result in the following: (1) The string, upon its release, will swing into an arc which will bring it into the alignment of the warped limbs; the string in turn will take the nock end of the arrow with it which would not be as it was aimed. Thus the arrow may go several feet to the right or left, depending upon the direction of the torsion of the limbs. (2) If the bow happens to have recurved tip ends which have gotten out of alignment with the string, the fault will be magnified as follows: (A) In drawing the string to full draw, the tips are unbent somewhat and in doing this they will tend to lean even more from alignment than in the normal braced position. (B) This increased torsion will tend to throw an arrow further from where it was aimed than if the bow had straight tips.

Caution: One should sight his bow from the tip ends occasionally when braced for shooting to make sure of the string alignment. This is important as it is easily corrected if it is corrected before it strains or breaks the ends. Improper bracing of a bow is often the reason that bow's tips are twisted. Allow an experienced archer to help you learn the proper method of bracing a bow.

Wax (bowstring): The new synthetic threads used for bowstring, as Fortisan and Dacron require a wax that will adhere to the string (something with a flexible bonding agent). For this purpose melted beeswax and latex rubber cement of equal parts may be blended together by stirring slowly. If poured into small paper cups to cool, a handy sized cake will be the result. This wax will not flip from the string even in extremely cold weather.

"Weeping Sheet": A booklet or sheet containing the final scores of a National or any other sort of archery tournament.

Weight of Arrows: All bows, depending upon their draw weight and cast, will shoot more efficiently with an arrow which is neither too light nor too heavy for that bow. (A) An arrow which is extremely light in weight would have to be extremely stiff in comparison to average arrow wood to shoot well; at the same time a light arrow would tend to drift easily with the cross winds or breezes. (B) An arrow which is too heavy would no doubt be too stiff as there is a relation of stiffness to weight and mass in all woods. Note: An arrow which is too stiff will tend to shoot to the left, while one too light will shoot to the right. (C) Since there is no set rule as to how heavy or how light an arrow can or should be to shoot efficiently from a bow of any given weight, one must, or should, try several sets to find arrows which will suit his own choice best. (The author shoots target arrows which are $\frac{5}{16}''$ diameter, 26" long by 11½ grains to the inch, approximately, when finished. He shoots close to a one-ounce hunting arrow; the same size and average weight shaft, but with the 1¾ inch extra shaft length required for hunting shafts. This extra shaft length, plus the weight of the broadheads, 125 grains, runs very close to an ounce. He shoots these arrows from a 53-pound hunting bow and shoots a 50-pound target bow for field practice and tournaments.

Weight Classes of Bows for Flight Shooting: (1) The N.A.A. has set up the following weight limit classes for the flight division contests: (a) Men 50, 65, 80 pound, unlimited and Foot bow, or the Free style classes. (b) Ladies 35, 50 pound, unlimited, and the Foot bow or Free style classes. (C) Juniors and intermediates, the same as ladies.

(2) The N.A.A. requires that all bows be checked by a tournament official not to exceed 24 hours prior to the shooting. This must be done with a scale which has been checked by a sealer of weights and measures or a person of equal authority, and the scale must have the stamp or certificate of this testing attached to it. A second scale may be used for additional checking if an archer so desires. (A) After one's equipment is qualified a sticker is attached to the face of the bow immediately below the handle. It shall include (1) the weight class of the bow, (2) the length of arrow to be used, (3) the exact weight of the bow at full draw of the arrow to be shot. (B) The full draw weight is taken at a

point which will render the tip or pile end of the flight arrow 1½ inches from the rear end of the arrow rest, or arrow track overdraw. (C) No bow which is in excess of two pounds over a class limit is allowable in that class under any circumstances.

Windage Adjustment: Making allowance for a cross or quartering wind by means of sight bar or point of aim adjustments. If the wind should be from the right, move the sight bar to the left; vice-versa for a left quartering wind. The opposite is true when using the point of aim.

Wind Checks: Fine splits or cracks which frequently appear upon the surface of a log due to twisting of the tree by the winds. Where these checks may not continue on into the heart wood, it is well to consider their full depth before cutting a piece of bow wood from a tree. The bark on a tree, if carefully studied, will give one a fairly good idea as to how much a log is actually twisted. Both of the faults should be taken into careful consideration to save time later.

Wind Flags: (Used specifically in target archery, not in field archery.) Small flags which shall be visible for 100 yards in order that an archer may determine the direction and the extent of a cross wind. These flags are usually directly behind a target and are usually not less than three feet, nor more than twelve feet above the uppermost scoring ring of the target face.

Wing Club: A club which comprises a membership of flight shooting archers.

Working Recurved Bow: (*See* "Bow types.") A bow of this type is one which has reverse bent tip ends usually of a very gentle type bend that actually unbend as a working part of the bow's action. This function tends to: (1) increase a bow's cast by having the snappy action of a short bow, and (2) to have the smoothness of draw characteristic of a long bow.

The ends of working recurved bows may vary from a very gentle bend such as the arc of a 24″ to 30″ circle down to the more popular curves with an arc more in relation to a 10″ to 12″ circle. The size of the arc of a circle to which a bow's curved ends may coincide is at times the reason for these expressions: "semi," "light," "medium," or "deep" working recurves,—and the more

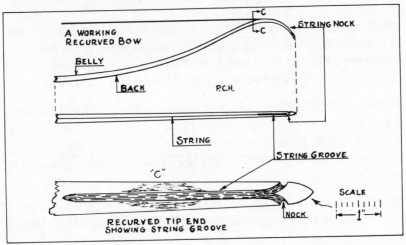

Fig. 29.—The top and side views of a working recurved bow. Sectional view "C" shows the string groove as it appears on the belly side of the curved tips. The more gentle the curve, the easier it is to align the tip ends.

nearly that the tip end reaches a complete quarter of the circle, the more severe would be the bow's action as to actual cast and shooting qualities.

The tip ends of a working recurved bow should never be allowed to get out of string alignment as this fault will not only spoil your aiming, but in time will ruin the bow. It pays to check a bow of this type frequently for bowstring alignment. (*See* "Warped Tips" and "Bowstring Alignment.")

Yew Wood: One of the finest of all bow woods. (*See* "Bow Woods" and "Taxus.")

Yielding to Target Mates: In large tournaments the archers are instructed to shoot three of their arrows, step back from the shooting line, or "yield," and allow their mates to do likewise. After the target mates have shot three arrows they must then "yield" and allow the first archers to resume shooting of their three remaining arrows. Again they "yield" to their mates who then complete shooting their remaining three arrows of the end. Each archer will have then shot a total of six arrows. (*See* "Shooting an end in National competition.")

York Round (American): This round, one of the most popular of all those shot in America by the men, is very often shot as a companion to the American Round. By doing so, an archer will shoot a maximum distance of 100 yards and the minimum of 40 yards. An archer who is capable of shooting a good York Round is usually destined to shoot a fine American Round due to the shorter distances in this round.

The York Round is shot as follows: 12 ends, or 72 arrows, from 100 yards; 8 ends, or 48 arrows, from 80 yards; 4 ends, or 24 arrows, from 60 yards.

This round, unlike the English York Round outlined under "Rounds, Target Archery," is shot from one end of the field in one direction only. The York Rounds require a total minimum walking distance of 4,160 yards.

York Round (English): (*See* "Rounds, Target Archery.") This round has been shot on occasions in the United States but is a very grueling one as it allows practically no rest from shooting or walking between the ends which are shot alternately from each end of the range. An end in this round constitutes but three arrows. The scoring must be kept on both ends of the range.

Young, Art: One of America's most outstanding archers and big game hunters. Many memorable trips were made which included Art Young and Dr. Saxton Pope during the late 1920's and early part of the 1930's. Art Young passed on in the fall of 1935. (*See* "Art Young Big and Small Game Award.")

"Zeroed In": An expression usually indicating one's readiness to start shooting for score or blood. Having one's sights or method of aiming to preciseness.

Zigzagging: An arrow which fishtails from side to side while in flight. This fault can be traced to any of the following situations: (1) A nock which is too tight on the string, thus starting into flight with a jerk from the string. (2) String braced too low to the bow. (3) A faulty release, as plucking the string. (4) An arrow which is considerably too stiff for the bow from which it is being shot. (5) An arrow that has improper fletching as would be the case of two right wing feathers and one left wing feather on the same arrow.

ARCHERY SHOPS AND SUPPLIERS

The following directory is for the convenience of the readers. (Neither the publisher nor the author will assume any responsibility for any error in these listings.) Many of the shops listed have catalogues which are available upon written request.

Abenaki Archery Co.
17 High Street
Kennebunk, Me.

Accurate Arrow Sales
1701 N. 21st Street
Milwaukee, Wis.

Ace Archery Tackle Co.
1611 Stanford Avenue
St. Paul 5, Minn.

Acme Wood Products Inc. (cedar shafts)
Myrtle Point, Ore.

Adkins, Gus R.
1125 Grace Street
Richmond 20, Va.

Albin Films (archery films)
1710 N. La Brea
Hollywood 46, Calif.

Alexandria Sport Shop, The (Aluminum Arrows)
1446 Duke Street
Alexandria, Va.

Allied Archery Co.
69 Margaret Street
Saranac Lake, N. Y.

Alray Archery Equipment Co.
139 Ewingville Road
Trenton 8, N. J.

Aluminum Arrows Industries
Dept. E
Bladen, Neb.

Ambroid Company (fletching cements)
Archery Division
Weymouth, Mass.

American Archery Co. (complete line)
2 Walker Avenue
Clarendon Hills, Ill.

Anderson Archery Sales Co.
(Jobbers — Wholesalers)
Grand Ledge, Mich.

Archer's Feather Supply Co., The
31 East 11th Street
New York, N. Y.

Archery Center (Bow quiver)
333 Fulton W.
Grand Rapids, Mich.

Archery Craftsman
Route 1
Coquille, Ore.

Archery Fibers Co. (thread)
356 Derby Avenue
Woodmere, N. Y.

Archery Headquarters of San Gabriel Valley
4528 N. Peck Road (P. O. Box 2093)
El Monte, Calif.

Archery Products Co.
515 S. Blair Street
Royal Oak, Mich.

Archery Research Co. (disappearing arrow rest)
Box 527 B
Abbe Road, R. D. 1
Elyria, O.

Archery Sales and Service, Inc. (complete line)
617 South State Street
Chicago 5, Ill.

The Archery Shack
4820 Hollywood Boulevard
Hollywood 28, Calif.

Archery Supply Shop
2800 Prescott Street
Saginaw, Mich.

Archery Trading Post, The (bow kits)
1327 So. Urbana
Tulsa 12, Okla.

Aro-Den
6516 Corkley Road
Baltimore 6, Md.

Arrowgraph Co. (arrow name labels)
947 So. Liberty
Alliance, O.

Arrowhead Archery Co. (wholesale suppliers)
Route 46
Denville, N. J.

Arrowhead Archery Shop
5 Calvary Road
Duluth, Minn.

Arrowhead Archery Shop
330 Southwest 28th Street
Oklahoma City, Okla.

Arrow-Head Plastics, Inc. (Seefab Bows)
318 East Superior Street
Duluth 2, Minn.

Arrowhead Sales (flint heads)
4588 So. Acoma Street
Englewood, Colo.

Arrowsmith (Broadheads)
Yulan, N. Y.

Arrowsmith
9716 Admiralty Drive
Silver Spring, Md.

Artex Mfg. Co. (archery shirts)
3433 Roanoke
Kansas City, Mo.

Atlantic Archery Shop
17-19 Chatham Avenue
Pleasantville, N. J.

Austin Archery Co. (Black wasp broadhead)
4513 E. Seneca
Des Moines 17, Ia.

Bacharach Rosin Co.
14 N. Howard Street
Baltimore, Md.

Bailey Arrows (arrow supplies)
3055 Clyde Park S. W.
Grand Rapids, Mich.

Bailey, H. L. (cross bows)
72 Summit Road
Elizabeth, N. J.

Baker, Jess K.
Ontario, Ore.

Bautro, Ted (complete line)
3219 Eastern Avenue
Baltimore 24, Md.

Bay Archery Supplies (bow strings)
1239 Mather Street
Green Bay, Wis. •

Baw Beese Archery Co.
No. 2 Orchard Street
Hillsdale, Mich.

Bazzurro, E.
5530 Netherland
Riverdale, N. Y.

B & B Mfg. Co. (glass shafts)
Box 611
Boulder, Colo.

Bear Archery Company (Complete line, mfrs. bows, arrows, leather goods)
Grayling, Mich.

Bear Archery Shop (complete line)
12238 Grand River
Detroit 4, Mich.

Beaver Sporting Goods Co. (bows)
1812 Laurel Street
Pittsburgh 33, Pa.

Beck's Archery Shop
1558 So. 9th Street
Noblesville, Ind.

Big Game Products, Inc.
Sportsman's Haven
Route 1
Alpena, Mich.

Bill's Tackle Shop
103 Beacon Avenue
Jersey City, N. J.

Bitzenburger, Henry A. (fletching jiggs)
800 East 4th Street
Los Angeles 13, Calif.

Blackhawk Archery Co.
2302 Gaylord Drive S.E.
Washington 37, D. C.

Black Lake Archery Shop, Inc.
Onway, Mich.

Black Palm Shop, The
Arthur, Ill.

Bloom, Walter (broadheads)
60 State Park Avenue
Salamanca, N. Y.

Blue Grass Archery Co.
635 So. Broadway
Lexington, Ky.

Bohning, R. A., Adhesives Co.
7328 Miller Road
Dearborn, Mich.

Bourquin, Bruce J.
170 North Black Horse Pike
Mount Ephraim, N. J.

Bow Archery Supplies
845 South Riverside
Medford, Ore.

Bow Art
6 Hillcrest Avenue
Massena, N. Y.

Bow Hunters Supply Shop (arrow supplies)
Glenwood, Minn.

Bowles, Duane (feathers)
722 Des Moines
Keokuk, Ia.

Bowman's Archery Supply, The
1126 Fourth Street, Northwest
New Philadelphia, O.

Bow String Fibers Co.
1103 Furth Road
Valley Stream, N. Y.

Boys Store—Hobby Shop
321 South 1st Street
San Jose, Calif.

Bracken, David (Buck lure)
R.F.D. 1
Ligonier, Pa.

Brahma Bow Co.
Box 432
Elkins, W. Va.

Braun, O. (spiral fletcher)
1100 Weiss Street
Saginaw, Mich.

Brooks, W. R., Inc. (Broadheads)
P. O. Box 2043
Fort Dearborn Stn.
Dearborn, Mich.

Bryson's Archery Shop
R. R. 5
Xenia, O.

Buccaneer Archery Co.
Box 6147
Corpus Christi, Tex.

Bull's Eye Archery Co.
472 Westminster Pl.
Lodi, N. J.

Burton, Guy L. (complete line)
357 — 3rd Street
Albany 6, N. Y.

Bushnell, D. P. Co., Inc. (Game
  Framer optics)
116 Bushnell Bldg.
Pasadena 1, Calif.

Cal-Tips (broadheads & field points)
Route 2, Box 846
San Marcos, Calif.

California Archery Supply Co. (feathers, wholesale)
1941 Central Avenue
El Monte, Calif.

Camouflage Products Co. (hunting
  apparel)
1287 E. Adams Street
Jacksonville, Fla., and
220 Lexington Avenue
New York 16, N. Y.

Carlisle Leathercraft (gloves)
R.F.D. 4 (Rt. 641) Newville
Carlisle, Pa.

Cascade Archery Co. (complete line)
4262 Northeast Killingsworth
Portland 13, Ore.

C & B Archery
P. O. Box 691
Fair Lawn, N. J.

Centaur Archery Co. (bows)
Glenshaw, Penn.

The Challenger (bows)
417 N. E. Broadway
Portland, Ore.

Chapen, Leon (yew wood)
1628 E. 8th Avenue
Albany, Ore.

Chernik, Larry (complete line)
3026 Evelyn Drive
Schenectady 3, N. Y.

Chiefs Archery Supply
2920 North Jackson
Wichita, Kan.

Chiodo, Ray
Box 791
Fruitland Park, Fla.

Chippewa Archery Shop
Mount Pleasant, Mich.

Clark, Howard D. (bowstrings)
1022 Chittock
Jackson, Mich.

C & M Archery (arrows)
26 Harrison Street
Janesville, Wis.

Clear Creek Archery Supply
Route 1
Pineville, Ky.

Coe Archery Shop (bows)
Otter Lake, Mich.

Craft Service
337 University Avenue
Rochester 7, N. Y.

Cravotta Brothers (jobbers and distributors)
3rd Street
East McKeesport, Penn.

Crescent Archery
71 Grand Avenue
Rockville Centre, N. Y.

Crestwood Archery Mfg., Inc.
2124 Surf Avenue
Brooklyn 24, N. Y.

C & S Archery Co. (Gum-Bak target
  faces)
1984 D Street
San Bernardino, Calif.

Crystal Lake Archery (feathers)
Beulah, Mich.

Cupp, Paul—Archery Supply (com-
  plete line)
P. O. Box 168
Joplin, Mo.

Custom Archery Supplies
900 E. Vince Street
Millville, N. J.

Custom Bow, Inc.
8220 Commercial
La Mesa, Calif.

Dana Bows
132 E. Myrrh Street
Compton, Calif.

Dandy Screw Products (fish heads)
4030 N. Kedizii Avenue
Chicago 18, Ill.

Darton Inc.
3261 Flushing Road
Flint 4, Mich.

Davco (bows)
3510 Manor Street
Los Angeles 39, Calif.

Davis Archery Co.
112 N. Fifth Street
Las Vegas, Nev.

Debro Products Co. (Embossed plastic archery accessories)
Box 164
Hawthorne, N. J.

De Francisco, Len, Archery Sales
405 W. Everett Street
Falconer, N. Y.

Desert Archery Shop (arrows)
1414 Alder
Richland, Wash.

Dexter and Bob's Archery Supplies (complete line)
29 Molton Street
Randolph, Mass.

Dillard & Wright Sporting Goods
516 Main Street
Springfield, Ore.

Dixie Sporting Goods Co.
211 N. 1st Street
Richmond, Va.

Doan, Harold
4334 North Adrian Road
Adrian, Mich.

Don's Archery Center
6900 N. Roberts Street
Portland, Ore.

Douglas Archery
241 Grand Avenue
Long Beach, Calif.

Drakes Archery Shop (bows)
Box 221
Lakeside, Calif.

Dunlap, Harry V. (cedar shafts)
1216 Saling Avenue
Medford, Ore.

Dunsdon, Les (bows)
18 Hamilton Avenue
Brantford, Ontario, Canada

Duoflex Archery Co.
2250 N. Tripp Avenue
Chicago 39, Ill.

Eagle Archery Mfg. Co. (broadheads and field points)
2550 W. 13th Street
Brooklyn 23, N. Y.

Eastern Sports (fletchers and trimmers)
42 Valley Road
Montclair, N. J.

Easton, James D., Inc. (24SRT-X aluminum arrow shafting)
15137 Califa Street
Van Nuys, Calif.

Eaton's Plastics, Inc. (slip on molded fletching)
2037 Oxmoor Drive
Dayton 3, O.

Eddings Archery Co. (bows)
McGregor, Ia.

Edgcomb-Hunter Hardwood Corp. (lemonwood staves)
53 Ann Street
New York, N. Y.

Edmonton Sporting Goods (complete line)
McLeod Bldg.
Edmonton, Alberta, Canada

Eggert, John L. (hunting heads—3 bladed)
607 Superior Avenue
Sheboygan, Wis.

E and H Archery (wooden arrows)
16525 Western Avenue
Gardena, Calif.

Eicholtz, Frank (Ultrabac—Glasface)
4032 El Cajon Boulevard
San Diego 3, Calif.

Elite Arrows
4129 Yorkshire
Detroit, Mich.

Emil Plastic (arrow displays)
8 Pearl Street
Plainview, N. Y.

Erickson, Ed
418—8th Street South
Moorhead, Minn.

Erno's Archery Shop (Bowstrings)
1291 Midland Road
Bay City, Mich.

Eugene and Company
P. O. Box 428
San Diego, Calif.

Everglad Archery Co.
455 Crystal Street
Akron, O.

Everglade Archery Co.
134 Northeast Avenue
Tallmadge, O.

Evergreen Archery Mfg. Co.
15621 N. East Street
Lansing 6, Mich.

Everitt, Martin (quick change heads)
25214 Tratoit Avenue
Roseville, Mich.

Ewing Products Company
1014 Burbank Blvd.
Burbank, Calif.

Falcon Archery Co. (custom bows)
P. O. Box 476
Atascadero, Calif.

Feather Merchants, The (feathers)
P. O. Box 2749 Powderhorn Station
Minneapolis 7, Minn.

Federal Instrument Corp. (Archery rangefinder)
Dept. A-1, 12-10 Bway.
Long Island City 6, N. Y.

Fieldcrest Archery Shop
Box 392
New Hope, Penn.

Fisk Archery
3409-3413 East Grant Rd.
Tucson, Ariz.

Fleetwood Archery Co. (complete
line)
3505 E. 39th Avenue
Denver 7, Colo.

Foster's Sporting Goods
8030 So. E. Harrold Street
Portland 6, Ore.

Francis Archery Co. (wholesale deal-
er)
Three Oaks, Mich.

Franklin, John
(Bow hunting stand)
5104 Harding
Dearborn, Mich.

Freeman's ("Bill") Archery Shop
(arrows)
840 The Alameda
San Jose, Calif.

Freid, Robert A. (arm quivers)
Cornell, Wis.

Fries, Joe (bows)
2934 Bank Street
Los Angeles 65, Calif.

Frontier Archery (complete line)
3032 Fifth Avenue
Sacramento, Calif.

Gabriel Archery Company
158½ N. Main Blvd.
Green Bay, Wis.

Garland's Gun & Archery Shop
6089 Highland Road, Route 7
Pontiac, Mich.

Gassman & Negley
1708 Fredricksburg Road
San Antonio 1, Tex.

Gebhardt, J. G. Co. (fletching jiggs)
230 Gralan Road
Catonsville 28, Md.

Geiger's Arrow-Way
Route No. 83 Bernville Road
Reading, Pa.

Geode Industries (tackle boxes)
106 W. Main Street
New London, Ia.

Glass Fiber Archery Co.
105 South 33rd Street
Newark, O.

Gobes Archery
Route 1
Little Suamico, Wis.

Goodwear Company
177 Flatbush Avenue
Brooklyn 17, N. Y.

Gopher Shooters Supply (wholesale
sporting goods)
Faribault, Minn.

Gordon Plastics, Inc. (facings & backings)
5328 Banks Street
San Diego 10, Calif.

Grand Rapids Archery Co.
2437 Brooklyn, Southeast
Grand Rapids 7, Mich.

Gray Archery Co. (arrows)
Box 11-B
North Ridgeville, O.

Grayling Film Service (archery movie
films)
Grayling, Mich.

Great Plains Aluminum Arrow Industries
Bladen, Neb.

Green, Dick, Archery (custom bows)
5418 Reseda Blvd.
Tarzana, Calif.

Greggs Tackle Shop
333 West 21st Street
Chester, Penn.

Gries Reproducer Corp. (points)
56—2nd Street
New Rochelle, N. Y.

Grimes Archery Co. (bows)
Pontiac Municipal Airport
Pontiac, Mich.

Grubbs, Earl (complete line)
5518 West Adams Boulevard
Los Angeles 16, Calif.

G & S Archery Co. (bow racks)
Suttons Bay, Mich.

Hamilton, Max (Plasti-fletch)
Route 1, Box 450
Flagstaff, Ariz.

Hamilton, "Stew," Archery Shop
8836 Broadway Avenue
Cleveland 5, O.

Hanley, Dale (complete line)
121 E. Pultney Street
Corning, N. Y.

Hartig's Arrow Shop (arrows)
Dept. A, 123 Winslow Place
Garwood, N. J.

Hecht, D. E. (feathers & processing)
80 University Place
New York 3, N. Y.

Heringson, J. E. (bow strings)
15644—47th Ave., South
Seattle 88, Wash.

Hesse's Archery Center
R. F. D. 1
Windsor, N. Y.

H-H Archery Shop (complete line)
612 E. Halliday
Pocatello, Ida.

Hiawatha Archery Co.
12934 N. W. 7th Ave.
Miami 50, Fla.

Highland Cabinet & Archery, or Paul
C. Hougham Cabinet Shop (custom
equipment)
P. O. Box 1287
Visalia, Calif.

Hill's Archery Supplies (3-bladed
broadheads and field points)
Box 35
Manitowish Waters, Wis.

Hi-Precision Co. (3-bladed broadheads)
Orange City, Ia.

Hit Archery Supply
Route 3
Archbold, O.

Hite Hardware, W. D. (bow sights)
Tecumseh, Mich.

Hi-Way Sports Center
Lincoln Highway
West Irwin, Penn.

Hobbies and Sports
1755 West 95th Street
Chicago 43, Ill.

Hobby-Horse Crafts (leather goods)
Wyandotte, Mich.

Hodek's, Jim, Archery Shop (bows)
Route 1, Box 51
Traverse City, Mich.

Howard Enterprises
415 W. Loma Alta Drive
Altadena, Calif.

Howard Hill Productions
8644 Foothill Blvd.
Sunland, Calif.

Howatt, Damon (arrows)
Route 8
Yakima, Wash.

Hoyt Archery Company
11510 Natural Bridge
Bridgeton, Mo.

Hunter, John A., Corp. (lemonwood)
53 Ann Street
New York 38, N. Y.

Hunter's Corner (Camouflage archery
suits)
117-14 Queens Blvd.
Forest Hills 75, N. Y.

Hunting Industries
1566 Wealthy, S. E.
Grand Rapids, Mich.

Idle Hour Sports (arrows)
488 W. Center Street
Marion, O.

Indian Archery & Toy Corp.
16–24 Clark Street
Evansville, Ind.

Indian Art Crafts (arrowhead jewelry)
Route 3, Box 145
Eugene, Ore.

Indianhead Archery Mfg. Co. (com-
plete line)
Box 303A
Lima, O.

Ingham Archery Supplies
Lanigan, Saskatchewan, Canada

Ivanhoe Manufacturing Co. (bows)
P. O. Box 249
Ludington, Mich.

Ja-Lea Company (Interchangeable
heads)
1826 Grovedale
Jackson, Mich.

Jalon, Paul (arrows)
4129 Yorkshire
Detroit, Mich.

Janssen, Paul
1903 Short Street
New Orleans, La.

Jayhawk Archery Co.
P. O. Box 1355
Wichita, Kans.

Jenkins, M. E. (bow quivers)
1736 Riverside Drive
S. Williamsport, Pa.

Jensen Archery & Leather
98 So. Main
Brigham City, Utah

Jones, H., Welding & Mfg. (Archery
glove)
7340 E. 11 Mile Road
Center Line, Mich.

Johnny G's Arrow Shop
408 W. Green Street
Orleans, N. Y.

Johnson Arrow Shop (complete stock)
Box 201
Kasson, Minn.

J. R. Products (bow quivers)
4040 State Street
Salem, Ore.

Ketzler Archery
817 Copeman Blvd.
Flint 4, Mich.

King Sport-Line Co. (leather accessories)
212 W. Colorado Blvd.
Pasadena, Calif.

Kinsey's Arrow Shop
Chocolate Avenue
Florin, Pa.

Kittredge Archery Co.
Box 386-A or 1421 Mission Street
South Pasadena, Calif.

Knipp, Chet
3016 Lindbergh Drive
Manitowoc, Wis.

Kodiak Archery Company (complete
line)
7418 Marlborough
Parma 29, O.

Kozloff, Nick (trophies and ribbons)
843 N. Sycamore
Rialto, Calif.

Kristal Kraft Sales (plastic arrow
nocks)
P. O. Box 813
Lexington, Ky.

Krohn's Archery Tackle Mfg. Co.
(complete line—wholesalers)
412 N. River Street
Ypsilanti, Mich.

Lafever Machine Shop (Mfgrs. of
target and field points)
240 N. 23rd Street
Springfield, Ore.

La Fond's Lightning Broadhead Co.
(broadheads-flat blade)
3747 Hunt Road
Lapur, Mich.

Lane, Bill (complete line)
6997 Clark Road
Paradise, Calif.

Lane Printing Co. (score cards)
Charleroi, Penn.

Lantow-Moore Spt. Goods
2nd & Franklin Streets
Napa, Calif.

Les' Arch-R-Mart (complete line)
4031 So. Main Street
Salt Lake City 7, Utah

Lilly Archery Co. (arrows)
Box 697
Waynesboro, Va.

Lindsey, A. L. (Wild call)
Box 543—B.H.
Brownwood, Tex.

Livingstone Archery Mfg.
8259 State Park Street
Centerline, Mich.

Lobo Archery Company (broadheads)
1114 Ortega
Carlsbad, N. Mex.

Lock-Groove Arrow Co.
4425 E. Virginia
Denver 22, Colo.

Locktite Company, Inc. (leathergoods
mfg.)
Gloversville, N. Y.

Longbow Archery
21719 Devonshire Street
Chatsworth, Calif.

Loomis Archery Co.
P. O. Box 4910
Portland, Ore.

Lozon Archery (fletcher)
131 Fourth Street
Marine City, Mich.

Lunsford, T.
Sutherlin, Ore.

Magger, Henry T. (small game heads)
Westfield, Wis.

Make-All Tool and Die Co. (hunting
heads)
1924 South 74th Street
West Allis, Wis.

Malhusen (fletching jiggs)
Spinning Wheel Lane
Stamford, Conn.

Mangrove Feather Co., Inc. (feathers)
42 W. 38th Street
New York 18, N. Y.

Marathon Line Co. (bowstrings)
Homer, N. Y.

Maraviov, Henry (target faces)
715 South Locust Circle
Compton, Calif.

Mar-Bow Archery Co. (aluminum
arrows)
P. O. Box 101
Pomona, Calif.

Marion Archery Supply Co. (Field
targets)
1231 N. Main Street
Marion, O.

Mark Archery Co., Inc.
204–11 Jamaica Avenue
Hollis, N. Y.

Marker, Edward-Archery (arrows)
49 Alsace Avenue
Buffalo, N. Y.

Marsh Archery
6015 Hammel Avenue
Cincinnati 13, O.

Martin, Fred M. Co. (Apollo bows)
540½ Broadway Avenue
Winnipeg, Manitoba, Canada

Martin's Archery Co. (cedar shafts)
1830 Etna Street
Klamath Falls, Ore.

May, W. A., and Green
35 South Court Street
Montgomery, Ala.

McCord's
776 So. Penna. Avenue
Winter Park, Fla.

McGreer Arrows (arrows)
253 N. 68th Street
Birmingham 6, Ala.

McKinney, M. L. (arrow shafts)
Oakland, Ore.

McMillan and Son (wholesale feather grinding)
5 Toledo Street
Seneca Falls, N. Y.

Medford Enterprises Inc. (arrow shafts)
P. O. Box 457
Phoenix, Ore.

Meigs, Tim (custom archery—complete line)
5015 Woodminster Lane
Oakland, Calif.

Metal Products, Archery Division (fishing head)
P. O. Box 143
Colvin Street
Syracuse, N. Y.

Michea, Louis R. (Arrow Stra-tin-er)
Taneytown, Md.

Midwestern Eng. & Mfg. Co. (Retractible blade fish heads)
711 Desoto Street
Ypsilanti, Mich.

Minero-Newcomb & Co., Inc. (dies for metal pins and buttons)
17 Maiden Lane
New York 38, N. Y.

Minisini, Albert (fishing head)
7832 W. Lorraine Place
Milwaukee 10, Wis.

Minnich, Charles (flight supplies)
1072–19th Avenue
Columbus 11, O.

Mohawk Sporting Equipment Co. (miscellaneous equipment)
736 Cleveland Street
Elyria, O.

Mon Valley Tubing Co. (aluminum shafting only)
630 Center Avenue
North Chorleroi, Pa.

Montana Fibre Glass
Box 1007
Reed Point, Mont.

Monte Vista Archery Co. (parallel hole plastic nocks)
8908 Tacoma Way
Tacoma, Wash.

Mohawk Archery Supply Co.
38 E. 4th Street
Huntington Station, N. Y.

Morris, Bervil (feathers)
3754 Verrue Ave.
Fresno, Calif.

Mullen, Roger's Archery Shop
5 Ellis Avenue
Bath, N. Y.

National Archery Mfg. Co. (tabs)
7200 Riverdale Road
Minneapolis 12, Minn.

National Trophy Sales, Inc.
75 W. Van Buren Street
Dept. AR2
Chicago, Ill.

Nat Lay, Inc. (rubber arrow fletchings)
359 N. 10th Street
Noblesville, Ind.

Nelson Archery
Milton, Wis.

New Haven Archery Co.
804 Bell Avenue
New Haven, Ind.

Newton Line Co., Inc. (Braided bow strings)
Homer, N. Y.

Nick's Archery Supply
4716 Troost Avenue
Kansas City 10, Mo.

Nielsen & Sons (tackle case kits)
St. Anthony, Ida.

Nor-Del Arrows
202 Tatnall Avenue
Norwood, Pa.

North American Archery
P. O. Box 7165
Seattle 33, Wash.

Northern Valley Archery
Box 322
Englewood, N. J.

Norway Archery Co. (cedar shafts)
Norway, Ore.

Northwest Archery Co.
19807–1st Avenue South
Seattle 88, Wash.

Northland Archery Shop
2232 Roslyn Ave.
Duluth, Minn.

Nu-Fletch
46 North Manchester Street
Brockton, Mass.

Ohio Archery Co.
497 South Diamond Street
Mansfield, O.

Orchard Industries, Inc. (Mfgrs. of fiberglas actionbow)
Hastings, Mich.

Osage Orange Archery Shop
R. R. 2
Urbana, Ill.

Outdoor Sports Mfg. Co. (bows)
Forestville, Conn.

Ozark Archery Co. (general)
R. R. #1
Garfield, Ark.

Ozark Woodcraft
Osage Beach, Mo.

P. & K. Products
P. O. Box 2074
Gary (Tolleston Station), Ind.

Pacific Archery (cedar shafts)
Bandon, Ore.

Pake Stephenson, Inc.
14 Commerce Street
Montgomery, Ala.

Panther Archery Co. (Unilaterally
woven fiberglas facing and backing)
1766 Jasmine Avenue
New Hyde Park, N. Y.

Parallel Plastics, Inc. (fiberglas facings and backings)
112 Poplar Avenue
Newark, O.

Park Archery
49 Alsace
Buffalo, N. Y.

Parker, Milfred J. (target faces)
6606 Hood Avenue
Huntington Park, Calif.

Paul Bunyan Archery Products
1307 Glenwood Avenue
Minneapolis 5, Minn.

Paul's Sporting Goods
Benson, Minn.

Pearson, Ben, Inc. (complete line)
Pine Bluff, Ark.

Peg Products Co. (non-burning fletch
trimmer)
Dept. A, 22 Willben Lane
Plainview, N. Y.

Perry Archery Sale
322 East Chevy Chase Drive
Glendale, Calif.

Peterman, Albert L.
1288 Dragoon
Detroit 9, Mich.

Phillips Archery Co.
200 Adams Street
East Tawas, Mich.

Pierce Model Works (tennon tools)
Finley Park, Ill.

Pierman, S. C. (fishing heads)
117 Huron River Drive
Belleville, Mich.

Pierson, E. Bud and Son (bows)
3109 Burnet Avenue
Cincinnati, O.

Politsch Hardware Co.
836 South 8th Street
Quincy, Ill.

Polyphase Mfg. Co. (bow stringer)
7 Dumont Street
Rochester 17, N. Y.

Polyvane Co.
Dept. 206A
1557 Green Bay Road
Highland Park, Ill.

Potter-MacQuarrie (complete line)
7500 Fair Oaks Boulevard
Fair Oaks, Calif.

Powell's, Rube, Archery Shop
128 N. Second Avenue
Chula Vista, Calif.

Precision Wood Parts Co. (shafts)
Box 506
Oakland, Oregon

Premier Thread Co. (Dacron string
kit)
Box 788
Pawtucket, Rhode Island

Pride Archery Co.
369–7th Avenue
New York 1, N. Y.

Provo Archery Feather Co. (feathers)
744 So. State Street
Orem, Utah

Pullens, Jim (supplies)
19 W. Pine Street
Lodi, Calif.

Rand, J. (archery decals)
101 Lilac Street
Bergenfield, N. J.

Rae-John, Archery Supplies
805 Middle
Leavensworth, Kans.

Reed Archery
2318–6th Ave., N.
Renton 2, Wash.

Reseda Sales & Manufacturing Co.
Box 787—Dept. D.
Reseda, Calif.

Rhodes-Polk-Mfgs. (Bows)
2227 E. 16th Street
National City, Calif.

Rich, Hugh (complete line)
1731 South Brand Boulevard
Glendale, Calif.

Rickard, Pete (Buck lure)
Box 22
Cobleskill, N. Y.

Riley Denton (custom arrows)
9406 Fruitland Avenue
Puyallup, Wash.

Riverton Archery Supply
518 Farnum Street
Beverly, N. J.

Robin Hood Archery Co.
215 Glenridge Avenue
Montclair, N. J.

Rogers Archery Shop
5 Ellas Avenue
Bath, N. Y.

Rogers Emblem Mfg. Co.
2450 So. Main Street
Los Angeles 7, Calif.

Roger's Trading Post
Main Street
Stepney, Conn.

Rohde, R. E. (fletchers)
3038 North Newhall Street
Milwaukee 11, Wis.

Rome Sporting Goods Mfg. Co.
104 John Street
Rome, N. Y.

Root Archery Co. (bows)
Route 3
Big Rapids, Mich.

Roper's Archery and Leather
6307 Mountain Blvd.
Oakland, Calif.

Rose City Archery Co.
Powers, Ore.

Rose Tool & Mfg., Inc.
12247 W. Fairview Avenue
Milwaukee 13, Wis.

Rota-Barb (fishing point and bow
reel)
655 N. E. Hood Avenue
Gresham, Ore.

Roving Arrow, The
1226 Oso
San Luis Obispo, Calif.

Sabre Archery Co. (complete line)
Catham, N. J.

Sanders Archery Co.
Cortland, N. Y.

Santa Monica Film Service (pig hunting movies)
1513 Bay Street
Santa Monica, Calif.

Santry, John H. (Ex-calibre broadhead)
7717 E. Quill Drive
Downey, Calif.

Saunders Archery Target Co. (target
mats)
Columbus, Nebr.

Saxon Company, The (Bows)
P. O. Box 224
LaGrange, Ill.

Schmid & Company (cross bows and
broadheads)
Dept. A-34, P. O. Box 213
Santa Barbara, Calif.

Scientific Archery Co.
532 West 19th Street
Costa Mesa, Calif.

Seattle Archery Distributors (wholesale and distribution)
22224 Highway 99
Edmonds, Wash.

Seminole Archery Sales
3522—9th Street
Tampa, Fl.

Shannon's Al, Archery Shop
1403 Jackson Avenue
Memphis, Tenn.

Sharp Archery Co. (Arrows)
1014 W. Burbank Blvd.
Burbank, Calif.

Shawnee Archery Shop
8652 Foothill Blvd.
Sunland, Calif.

Shawsheen Archery Co. (broadheads)
Box 176
Winchester, Mass.

Sherwood Forest Equipment Co.
(aluminum arrows)
2105–7 W. Liberty Avenue
Pittsburgh 26, Pa.

Shumaker Archery Co. (broadheads)
R. R. #15 Wood Avenue
Fort Wayne, Ind.

Siskiyou Cedar Products
Cave Junction, Ore.

S. & J. Archery Sales (Smithwick
bow)
10945 Burbank Blvd.
North Hollywood, Calif.

Smith Archery
816 Malzahn Street
Saginaw, Mich.

Smith, John D.
4401 East Avenue
Rochester 18, N. Y.

Sneed, Evelyn (bow strings)
20026 Kittridge Street
Canoga Park, Calif.

Snyder, Bob
2506 Loomis Street
LaCrosse, Wis.

Song Bird Archery Shop
Box 54
Clinton, Pa.

Southern Oregon Archery Supply
(cedar arrow shafts)
Kerby, Ore.

Sporting Goods, Foster
800 S. E. Harold Street
Portland, Ore.

Sporting Goods—Lanton & Moore
2nd and Franklin Streets
Napa, Calif.

Sportsman's Haven
Route 1
Alpina, Mich.

Sportsmans Paradise
227 West Philadelphia Street
Whittier, Calif.

Sportsmen Accessories, Inc. (fiberglas bows)
Beacon, N. Y.

Sportsmen, The
P. O. Box 2115
Santa Ana, Calif.

Stalker Archery Co., The
Clintonville, Wis.

Stalker, Tracy (book)
G4221 Springfield
Flint 7, Mich.

The Stafford Company (feathers)
Albia, Ia.

Stag Mountain Archery Co.
2042 Longmount
Boise, Ida.

Steiner's Archery Shop (bows)
2986 Fifth Avenue
Huntington, W. Va.

Stettler, R. A. Archery Co.
P. O. Box 62
Atascadero, Calif.

Stemler, L. E., Co. (complete line)
Manorville, N. Y.

Stevenson's Products, Inc. (Bow quiver)
Wellsboro, Pa.

Stream-Eze (fibreglass bows and
arrows)
Charlevoix, Mich.

Storer, W. A.
720 N. Federal Ave.
Mason City, Ia.

Super-Cedar Arrow Shaft Co.
1550 N. Irving Street
Coquille, Ore.

Straubel Mfg. Co.
Route 3, Box 505
Racine, Wis.

Sturr, Harold
140 S. Middle Neck Road
Great Neck, N. Y.

Sunline Plastics (fiberglas arrows)
Route 1
Hastings, Mich.

Sur-Nock Materials Co.
P. O. Box 4807
Kansas City, Mo.

Sweetland, William E. (Forgewood
and Battleshafts)
2441 Hilyard Street
Eugene, Ore.

Tarbell Archery Co. (custom bows)
P. O. Box 265
Cucamonga, Calif.

T. & S. Archery (field points)
P. O. Box 28
Freeport, Ill.

T. and V. Archery Sales
2225–24th Street
Fort Huron, Mich.

Tessier Bros. (spine tester)
622 Smith Street
Schenectady 5, N. Y.

Texas Feathers, Inc. (feathers)
Box 285
Brownwood, Tex.

The Old Master Crafters Co. (bow
kits and laminations)
P. O. Box 241
Waukegan, Ill.

The Outdoor Sports Mfg. Co. (fiberglas bows)
Forestville, Conn.

The Riverton Archery Supply
P. O. Box 209
Riverton, N. J.

The Staghorn Archery Co.
Merrill, Wis.

The String Shop (Bowstrings)
Eldorado 2, Ill.

Thomas Archery Shop
Route 2
Filer, Ida.

Thurlow Glove Company (gloves,
bow cases)
100 N. E. Union Avenue
Portland 14, Ore.

Thomas' Textile & Sporting Goods
416 Sherman
Couer d'Alene, Ida.

Thompson, Joseph D. (lefthand bows)
Garrison Forest Road
Owings Mills, Md.

Thunderbird Arrows (Dick Ellinger)
752 Sweet Home Road
Eggertsville 21, N. Y.

Tillmark Archery (complete line)
Main Street, North
Newmarket, Ontario, Canada

Trail-Eze Archery Co.
P. O. Box 2043 M. B. Sta.
Dearborn, Mich.

Tri-State Archery Corp. (Custom
bows)
16-18 River Street
Danbury, Conn.

True Arrow (aluminum arrow
straightener)
21–64–33rd Street
Astoria 5, N. Y.

True Flight Arrow Company
Monticello, Ind.

Trueflight Manufacturing Co. (feather
grinding, and brush buttons)
Manitowish Waters, Wis.

Tru-Rest Products (Bow and arrow
racks)
Bramer Road
Soders, N. Y.

Turner Brothers (aluminum shafts)
Wellington, O.

United Archery Co. (Bows)
Div. of Stream-Eze Inc.
Charlevoix, Mich.

Universal Targets (target archery and field faces, score cards, etc.)
525 North Noble Street
Chicago 22, Ill.

Uncle Rogers Archery Shop
2117 Taraval
San Francisco 16, Calif.

Van-Albin Feathers
Box 5001
Boise, Ida.

Van Der Kogel, A. F. (Seefab distributor)
78 Woodedge Road
Plandome, N. Y.

Viking (complete line)
1874 Market Street
San Francisco, Calif.

Viky-Jim Products
7663 Evergreen
Detroit 28, Mich.

Wahl Arms Co. (Medals)
FA65 Bogata, N. J.

Walsh, Larry
1114 Dibb Street
Bremerton, Wash.

Walt Whittum (Decals)
191 Chestnut Street
Springfield, Mass.

Ward's Archery Shop
700 Crowslanding Road
Modesto, Calif.

Warner's Custom Archery
61 Church Street
Millville, N. J.

Warrior Archery Mfg. Co. (arrow points)
1833 South Kinnickinnic Avenue
Milwaukee 4, Wis.

Warwick Archery Specialties Co.
1123 Fullerton Avenue
Chicago 14, Ill.

Waterman, Jim, Custom Arrows
28 Van Horn Street
West Springfield, Mass.

Wayside Printers (Rigid target faces)
Pottstown, Pa.

Webb's Archery Supplies
809 Carrier Parkway
Grand Prairie, Tex.

Weber, Del (feathers and custom feather grinding)
809 Chehalem Street
Newberry, Ore.

Weems Wild Call
P. O. Box 7261
Fort Worth 11, Tex.

Wellman Archery Company
365 Elm Street
Wadsworth, O.

Western Archery
3024 Ashby Avenue
Berkeley, Calif.

Western Archery Mfgrs. (complete line)
288–4th Avenue
Kamloops, B. C., Canada

West's Archery
9219 California Street
South Gate, Calif.

Whiffen, L. C., Co., Inc. (complete line)
209 West Wells Street
Milwaukee 3, Wis.

White, Wilson I., Mfg. Co. (Manufacturers of bows)
P. O. Box 86
Lakeside, Calif.

Wiese, Carl H., Archery Co.
152–36th Street
Ogden, Utah

Wildwood Archery Co. (complete line)
P. O. Box 314
Michigan City, Ind.

Williams, Colonel
1220 Burbank Blvd.
Burbank, Calif.

Wilson-Allen Corp. (nock locks)
Box 201
Windsor, Mo.

Wilson Brothers (endless string jigg)
P. O. Box 917 Commercial Station
Springfield, Mo.

Wonderland Archery Co. (custom arrows)
1335 Court Street
Redding, Calif.

Woodcraft Equipment Co. (manufacturers of York equipment)
Independence, Mo.

Woodcraft Hobby Stores (bow sights)
903 W. Lake Street
Minneapolis, Minn.

Woodsmen Archery Supplies
541–2 FPHA
W. LaFayette, Ind.

Woody's Shaft Shop (arrow shafts)
Rogue River, Ore.

Wright, George (Arrow straightener)
Box 3704
Detroit 37, Mich.

Yo-Bo Archery Co.
Houtzdale, Pa.

York Arrows, Ltd. (aluminum arrows)
P. O. Box 208
Mar Vista, Calif.

R. C. Young Co.
3602 Michigan Avenue
Manitowoc, Wis.

INDEX